Creating Decorative Fabrics

in 1/12 scale

Creating
Decorative
Fabrics
in 1/12 scale

JANET STOREY

GUILD OF MASTER CRAFTSMAN PUBLICATIONS

First published 2002 by
Guild of Master Craftsman Publications Ltd,
166 High Street, Lewes,
East Sussex, BN7 1XU

ISBN 1 86108 264 9
A catalogue record of this book is available
from the British Library
Photographs by Anthony Bailey, GMC Publications Photographic Studio

Designed by Kevin Knight
Cover design by Kevin Knight
Typeface: Joanna MT and Rotis Sans Serif

Colour Separation by Viscan Graphics, Singapore

Printed and bound by Sun Fung Offset Binding Co. Ltd, China

CONTENTS

Introduction

There comes a time in the life of every miniaturist when the search for greater accuracy in textiles becomes frustrating. Toiles-de-Jouy and William Morris prints, to name but two, do not exist in miniature. I hope to show you ways of achieving more accuracy in, and adding individuality to, your work.

My interest in fabrics and fittings is lifelong. My mother taught me to knit and crochet before I started school and as a five year old I was making clothes for my dolls. At high school my needlework teacher told me I should take up typing – I think this was because I found school needlework such a crashing bore. But even she couldn't damage my enthusiasm.

Later I became interested in how fabrics and fibres were created. I learnt to spin and then to colour the wool and silk that I was producing. Discovering dolls' houses and miniatures increased the range of techniques open to me. The most important lesson I have learnt is that nothing is impossible, and nothing is as difficult as it first appears.

My aim is to give you a gentle introduction to some of the techniques available – a few very old and a few new. You will probably already have most of the equipment and materials in your home, and if not, they are all easily obtained. Some of the techniques are of the kitchen stove and table type, others of the comfy armchair. I hope you enjoy trying them out and that your results encourage you to go on and learn more.

It is not always necessary to do things exactly as described; it is a final effect you are aiming for, particularly in miniatures, and you need only do as much as is necessary to get there. But remember, it is often the finishing details that lift a project from the ordinary to the extraordinary, so do not skimp on these. Think a little laterally. If you don't have what you need, think of what can be used as a substitute; a clotheshorse can make a fine weaving frame, for example.

Above all, do have fun.

Janet Storey
January 2002

Natural dyes

It is my hope to introduce you to the world of colour that has been gifted us by nature. I have given instructions for a limited range of colours, leaving out any complicated chemistry. To simplify what can be a very complex subject, I have only provided the information you need to get results. The methods described will produce the maximum results for the minimum financial outlay. I hope they will encourage you to experiment with other dyestuffs and mix different batches of dyes to produce new colours.

To keep things simple I have concentrated on wool. Wool has a great affinity for natural dyes. Silk has a similar affinity but will not take on as intense a colour. Cotton and linen require a special process to make them accept dye. Synthetic fibres have no affinity for natural dyes and, in fact, aren't very receptive to many chemical dyes.

DYESTUFFS

The only way to get historically accurate colours in your needlework is to use the same dye sources as were used in the originals; for pre-nineteenth century designs, this means natural dyes.

Prior to the sixteenth century, wool that had been spun in the home was either dyed there or sent to the professional dyers' guilds. It was then returned to the home for weaving, knitting or needlework. Occasionally the newly dyed wool was sent on to the weavers' guild to be made into cloth before being returned for use in clothing and furnishings.

Only with the invention of the spinning jenny did the processes of spinning, dyeing and weaving become centralized and mechanized.

Until the early nineteenth century, only natural dyes were available for colour application; the whole economy of some countries was built upon the growth of dye plants. However, by the middle of the century, natural dyes had largely been superseded by the new, synthetic coal-tar dyes.

Although William Morris, a designer, craftsman and important figure in the Arts and Crafts movement, successfully reintroduced natural dyes at his studios at the close of the nineteenth century, synthetic dyes, being less labour intensive and cheaper to produce, were here to stay. Despite this, plant dyes have never really lost their appeal: the colours are glorious or subtle and best of all, they are always harmonious – there are no clashing colours in nature.

EXAMPLES OF THE SUBTLE COLOURS THAT CAN BE ACHIEVED USING NATURAL DYES

3

Madder powder

Only the root of the madder plant is used to obtain dye; a fresh root will give a stronger colour than dried. Madder is available as a powder or chopped, in which form it is known as madder chips. I have used both powder and chips and have yet to decide which is best. The powder is difficult to strain from the dye bath and sticks to the wool, but with it colour extraction is easier; chips require a longer soak and longer cooking to extract the dye.

Madder was cultivated for centuries. The ancient Egyptians were using it as a dye around 2000BC and it was being cultivated by the Turks around 1000 years ago; records are a bit vague as it was a closely guarded secret. Madder formed the basis of a flourishing industry in the Netherlands, at its peak during the fifteenth century. The introduction of synthetic dyes, in the latter half of the nineteenth century, killed off this industry, damaging the economy of the Netherlands quite severely as a result.

Colours produced
Brown, red and orange

Cochineal

This dye is obtained from the bodies of the female *Dactylopius coccus* beetle, native to South America. In the sixteenth century the dye was introduced to Europe by the Spanish, who learnt the technique of obtaining it from indigenous tribes. At the time this gave madder growers cause for concern, but the cost of cochineal kept the madder industry from going into decline at this time.

The beetles are first dried, either in the sun or in an oven. Those dried in the sun are known as 'Negra' and those dried in an oven as 'Silver'. The Negra give the best colour. Nearly 75,000 beetles are needed to produce 450g (1lb) of cochineal.

Only a very small amount of dye is needed to give a good, strong colour. Don't be tempted to use more than you need: you will end up dyeing bags of wool just to use it up.

Colours produced
Red, purple and pink

MADDER POWDER

COCHINEAL

Brazil wood

Brazil wood is a red wood obtained from tropical trees of the genus *Caesalpinia*, found principally in North and South America. The dye, of the same name, is found in the woody trunk and branches.

Colours produced

Black, Bordeaux, blue-grey and dull pink

BRAZIL WOOD

Dyer's-weed (broom)

This plant, native to northern Europe, has been used as a dye plant for many centuries.

Colours produced

Yellow and yellow-green

DYER'S-WEED

Onion skins

Onion skins produce a fast dye, even without a mordant. They produce a good range of colours and are also useful for mixing with other dye liquids to obtain new colours.

Colours produced

Orange and yellow

ONION SKIN

Logwood

Logwood comes from the heartwood of *Haematoxylon campecianum*, a tree native to South America. It is a very powerful dye and will stain anything it touches, even without a mordant.

Colours produced

Blue, violet-grey and black

LOGWOOD

AMOUNTS REQUIRED
Madder powder 115g (4oz)
Logwood 85g (3oz)
Dyer's-weed (broom) 60g (2oz)
Cochineal* 1tsp
Brazil wood 85g (3oz)
Onion skins** 115g (4oz)

◎◎

* The minimum quantity of cochineal that you can buy is 25g (approx. 1oz)

** These are available free from your local greengrocer or supermarket, but ask for permission first!

Processing the dye materials

Without a preservative, dyes cannot be stored in liquid form. In dry form, as obtained from the supplier, they can be stored indefinitely in an airtight container. As an extra precaution, store in a dark place.

Pans made from aluminium, copper, tin or iron will shed tiny amounts of metal into each dye bath. These tiny particles affect the processing of dye materials. The effects can be utilized but the results are unpredictable, so it is better to use neutral, non-porous vessels, for example, enamel-coated or stainless steel. The implements you use should also be made of a neutral material such as wood, plastic or glass.

Gather together as many jars, jugs and other non-metallic containers as you have dyestuffs. These should have a capacity of no less than 250ml (½pt). Use one container per dyestuff.

Place 115g (4oz) of onion skins in a jar, cover them with warm water and set aside. It isn't necessary to seal the jars, and in some cases this would be hazardous. Plant materials have a tendency to ferment and this fermentation causes the release of gases which, in a sealed container, could cause it to explode. Do the same with all your dye materials with the exception of cochineal. Crush this into the smallest particles you can before placing it in the jar and covering with water. This will greatly speed up the rate of dye extraction – and there is nothing worse than looking at a jar full of re-hydrated dead beetles and then having to squeeze the dye out of them! Remember to label each jar.

The colour from madder improves after a longer soak, particularly if it is allowed to ferment. Leave it for a minimum of three days, and use it at the last moment to get the best results.

MORDANTS

Wool will take up any dye but, unfortunately, the dye won't always stay. As soon as the wool is rinsed, the dye will leave it and colour the rinsing water. Any dyes that do stay in wool are liable to fade in light, wash out in laundering and rub off during use.

To combat this a mordant must be used. Mordants are chemicals that bind dyes to wool. Often a number of mordants can be used with the same dyestuff to produce totally different colours, for example, logwood will produce blue, violet, grey, purple and black according to the mordant used. In the past such wonderful ingredients as urine and dung were used – and they worked! However, I promise you we will only be using conventional mordants here.

Alum

This, the most popular mordant, has a long history, being known and used in ancient Egypt. It is often combined with cream of tartar, without which the resultant colour would be duller and more muted. It brightens, evens and fixes the final colour.

ALUM

Copper

This is another ancient mordant. Adding vinegar will reduce the amount of copper required and also increase its colourfastness. Use sensible precautions when handling copper; wear gloves, don't use food preparation vessels for mixing, and clean up any spills immediately.

COPPER

Chrome

This is light-sensitive when in solution so dissolve only enough for immediate use. If you add chrome to a yellow bath it will become orange or rust-coloured. It makes wool feel soft and silky and gives it a nice lustre.

CHROME

Iron

This was one of the first mordants to be discovered, in all likelihood because water being used to wash wool was contaminated with iron salts. It is usually used after dyeing to sadden (darken) colour or tone it down. An iron nail makes a good substitute.

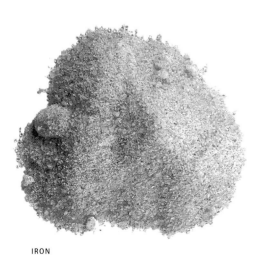

IRON

Tin

Tin is another mordant used at the end of dyeing; it will intensify and bloom (brighten) colours. If used with cochineal a bright scarlet is obtained.

TIN

ASSISTANTS TO MORDANT

In addition to these metals, you will also need a few household chemicals, including cream of tartar and vinegar (white, although malt can be useful for dark colours), as assistants to mordant. Another assistant to mordant is baking soda, which will change yellow to yellow-green. Salt will soften colours and slightly retard the rate of dye take-up. A salt rinse after dyeing will help to fix the dye.

APPLYING A MORDANT

There are four methods of applying a mordant to your wool: pre-mordant, simultaneous mordant, using the dye pot as a mordant and saddening or blooming. The dye baths given in this chapter use simultaneous mordant, saddening and blooming techniques. Alum is the mordant used for every dye bath, with other mordants and assistants added to modify the resultant colours.

Pre-mordant

Here, mordants are used before dyeing. The treated wool can either be used immediately, dried and stored for future use, or stored damp in a plastic bag. It can be kept in this way for up to three days without detriment; such storage will often brighten the final colour.

Simultaneous mordant

Following this method, the mordant is dissolved in the dye bath.

Dye-pot mordant

If you use an aluminium, copper or tin pan as a dye bath, the dye will take up some of the metallic element allowing you to either omit the mordant or drastically reduce the amount used.

Saddening or blooming

To produce these effects, the correct mordant, or assistant to mordant, is added to the dye bath just before the end of dyeing, producing a rapid reaction. This is very useful when you are using iron or tin, as these metals will make wool feel hard and brittle if it is left for too long in the dye bath. If you use this technique you must not let the dye bath boil, as boiling increases the hardening effect of iron and tin.

GLAUBER'S SALT (LEFT) AND CREAM OF TARTAR
(RIGHT) ARE BOTH USED AS ASSISTANTS TO MORDANT

THE PROCESS OF DYEING

When you are preparing a number of colours, I recommend that you set aside as many days as you have dyestuffs and concentrate on one dyestuff per session. It is important to keep an accurate record of the process that you have used and a sample of the coloured wool. This will be invaluable if you want to repeat the colour. Dye enough wool to complete your project: it is virtually impossible to obtain the exact shade again. The quantities I have given should be enough to complete several projects.

Winding the wool

The wool must be wound into skeins of a suitable size for dyeing – every craft has its tedious part. If your wool is in a hank (a large skein), then you must first wind it into a ball. Use something as a core to wind onto; either a polystyrene ball, a tightly wound ball of waste wool (perhaps knitting wool), or anything else you have to hand – even a clean eraser or tennis ball will do. If you are a spinner, you probably have a swift or a skein winder, but if you aren't and don't, loop the hank over the back of a chair or between the hands of a willing helper.

Take a piece of balsa wood or very stiff card, 450 × 70 × 6mm (18 × 3 × ¼in), and cut a slit at one end. Anchor the end of the wool in the slit and wind it around the wood about 50 times. This will give a skein of approximately 15g (½oz); if it doesn't, adjust the number of winds as required. Tie the two ends together but do not remove the wool from your winder yet. Take one end around the skein and tie it loosely to the other end before cutting the thread free. Cut three short lengths – around 10cm (4in) – to make three further loop ties at equal distances around the skein.

Remove the skein from your winder, twist it and fold it in half, allowing it to fold in on itself. Set the skein aside. You will need at least 94 skeins to complete all of the dye batches given here.

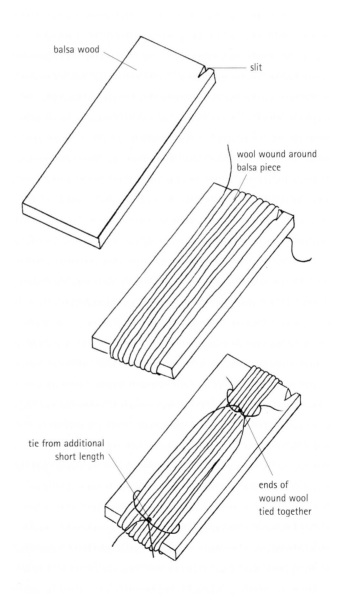

balsa wood

slit

wool wound around balsa piece

tie from additional short length

ends of wound wool tied together

A SIMPLE, IMPROVISED SKEIN WINDER

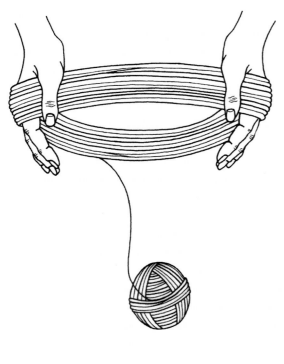

UNDYED WOOL IS GENERALLY BOUGHT AS A LARGE CONE OR HANK AND MUST BE WOUND INTO SMALLER SKEINS FOR DYEING

WINDING THE WOOL INTO SKEINS

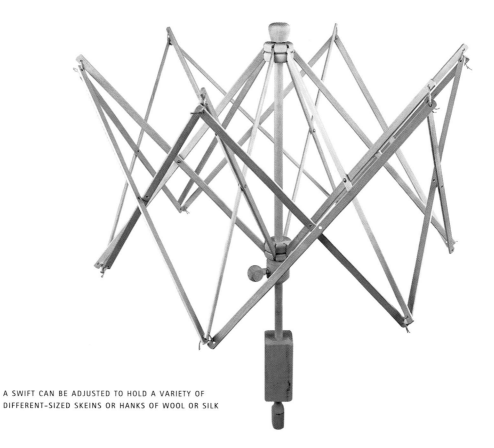

A SWIFT CAN BE ADJUSTED TO HOLD A VARIETY OF DIFFERENT-SIZED SKEINS OR HANKS OF WOOL OR SILK

A SKEIN WINDER WILL MAKE THE JOB OF WINDING THE WOOL EASIER

Washing the wool

Sheep's wool is made waterproof by lanolin, also known as grease and wool fat. All wool is spun 'in the grease', as washing before spinning makes it very difficult to form a thread; most regular hand spinners have very soft hands. Mill-spun wool, however, is degreased and has any debris removed before it is spun. For wool treated in this way, processing oil is used to facilitate the spinning. New wool must be washed in detergent (scoured) before dyeing, as grease or oil will prevent the dye penetrating the fibres. I find it better to wash my wool and prepare the dyestuff the day before I begin to dye. This way I can be absolutely sure that the water has penetrated every fibre of wool. This enables the dye to penetrate the wool more easily, and gives a more even colour take. Preparing the dyestuff the day before helps soften the plant fibres prior to cooking, allowing increased colour extraction.

While the dyestuffs are soaking, wash your previously wound skeins. Wash all of them: the wool will not be harmed by keeping it wet for a few days, and this storage will enhance the final colour.

Use a good wool wash preparation, detergent-based not soap-based, in hand-hot water. A soap-based preparation will not remove the grease but, being the principal ingredient for felt making, will cause the wool to felt. This is why woollen clothing washed in soap, no matter how much care is taken, will eventually felt. Rinse well at the same temperature. Do not wring or twist the wool – this may cause it to mat or tangle, making it impossible to unwind – but gently squeeze out the excess water. Leave the wool wet until you are ready to dye it. Every fibre must be wet before it is placed in the dye bath: this will help the dye to penetrate evenly.

Always aim to add cold, wet wool to a cold dye bath. If the dye bath is already hot, place the wool in a separate pan of cold water and bring this to the same temperature as the dye bath. The wool can then be lifted from the heated pan and placed directly into the dye bath. There is no need to squeeze out the excess water from this wool; it will not affect the final colour. Adding cold wool to an already hot dye bath will cause it to shrink and mat.

Drying the wool

With all your dyeing finished, the wool can now be dried. You can leave the wool to dry naturally if you have the time, but it will drip everywhere if it is not spun first. You must not use a tumble dryer for this, as the heat would cause the wool to shrink and felt, but you can use a spin dryer if you place the wool in a laundry bag or old pillowcase.

The skeins benefit from being slightly stretched while drying. Place the wool over a length of dowel and tie the dowel to your washing line or clotheshorse. Insert a second length of dowel into the bottom of the skeins; you can tie a weight to the centre of this.

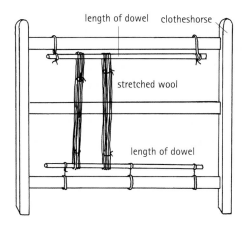

STRETCHING THE WOOL AS IT DRIES

General guidelines

🐦 Aim to add the wool to a cool dye bath and bring them both to temperature. After the required processing times, allow the wool to cool in the dye bath. When you are doing a lot of exhaust colours (see below), this obviously isn't practical. As an alternative, you can remove the wool and place it in the rinsing water, but this must be at the same temperature as the dye bath. The temperature of the wool can be lowered gradually with subsequent rinsing.

🐦 Always ensure that there is sufficient water in the dye bath for the wool to 'swim' freely – the more the better. A lot of water will not dilute the colour, but will prevent hot spots and scorching, which cause the wool to become brittle and discoloured. In any pan there are some areas that will be hotter than others. As with cooking, anything that comes into contact with these hot areas will stick if insufficient water is used. In addition, as the temperature of the water around these areas will be hotter, the rate of dye take-up by the wool will be affected, causing a patchy finish.

🐦 While you are processing one batch of wool, a second pan can be heating the next batch to temperature. This will then be ready to go into the dye bath when the first skeins come out, speeding up production dramatically.

🐦 The most important thing to remember is not to shock the wool with sudden temperature changes or excess agitation in the dye bath. If this happens you could end up with a very nicely coloured skein of felt or wool, but one which won't unwind. Wool fibres have scales which are all tightly closed. When wool is shocked, by being added cold to a hot dye bath or by over-agitation, these scales open and become tangled with scales from other strands, effectively locking together. This is known as felting.

🐦 A dye bath can become drained of colour by successive dips. This will result in paler shades of the same colour, known as exhaust colours. These are very useful in needlework.

TO CONTINUE...

The basic procedures for all dye plants are much the same. It is the mordant that modifies the colours and extends the range; in some instances the mordant can produce totally different colours from the same plant. I hope I have inspired you to go on and experiment with other natural materials.

There are many plants that are known to yield good dye colours. Walnut husks and henna give good browns, and weld will produce wonderful yellows. However, several species of wild flower are threatened because of over-collection. In Britain, under the Wildlife and Countryside Act (1981), it is illegal to dig up any wild flower without the permission of the landowner. Some species receive further protection under this Act and must not be damaged in any way. In the past lichens were widely used for dyeing. They are very slow growing and have been badly affected by air pollution. In some parts of the country they are now very rare and should not be collected. Be very careful what you pick. There are more than enough cultivated dye plants available without depleting our natural environment.

Precautions

Nature, being a little cruel, has added some risk to her gifts. Some of her dyestuffs and most of her mordants are toxic. However, as you will be using such tiny quantities of both dye and mordant, and providing you take sensible precautions, the risk to your health and the environment are negligible.

❦ Wear rubber gloves of good quality and fit

❦ Never use the same equipment for food preparation

❦ Always clean up spills as they happen

❦ Have a thorough clean-up after you have finished

A HUGE RANGE OF COLOURS CAN BE PRODUCED USING ONLY NATURAL DYES

EQUIPMENT AND MATERIALS

It is likely that most of the necessary equipment will already be in your kitchen; if not, it can be bought very cheaply from junk and charity shops.

Bucket, plastic or enamel

Bowls, small plastic or enamel × 2

Large pans, stainless steel or enamel × 2 (I use an old jam pan and the base of a pressure cooker for sample dyeing and a Baby Burco for batch dyeing)

Measuring jugs, 2l (3½pt) × 2

Plastic colander

Nylon sieve

Well-fitting, good-quality rubber gloves × 2 pairs

Spoons, wooden or plastic, or lengths of smooth dowel

Scales

Measuring spoons

Pestle and mortar or strong plastic bag and heavy implement

Balsa strip, 450 × 70 × 6mm (18 × 3 × ¼in)

Wool of your choice, a minimum of 1.5kg (3lb 5oz)

Detergent-based wool washing liquid

Dyestuffs:
onion skins/cochineal/ brazil wood/ dyer's-wood/ logwood/madder

Mordants:
alum/copper/tin/iron/chrome

Assistants to mordant:
cream of tartar/ white vinegar/salt/chalk

KEY TO TEMPERATURES

Just simmering: 88–90°C (190°F)
Simmering: 91–95°C (200°F)
Boiling: 100°C (212°F)

MOST OF THE ITEMS NEEDED ARE EVERYDAY KITCHEN EQUIPMENT

SESSION ONE | ONION SKIN

In this first session you will be dyeing for three colours, using six skeins of wool each.

First bath

Mordant: alum
Assistant: salt

1 Place the previously soaked onion skins, together with the water in which they were soaked, in your largest pan. Cover the skins generously with cold water. Place the pan over a high heat and bring to the boil, then reduce the heat until the pan is simmering. Leave to simmer for 60 minutes.

2 Strain off the onion skins and discard, then pour the liquid, in equal amounts, into three separate jugs and return one-third to the pan. Top this up with cold water until the pan is two-thirds full.

3 Dissolve 30g (1oz) of alum in 1tbsp boiling water and add this to the dye bath, stirring well. The bath should now be cool enough – barely warm – to immerse the first two skeins of wool. If not, fill your second pan with cold water and immerse all six skeins. Bring this pan to the same temperature as the dye bath. Leave the wool to stay warm in this until you are ready to dip it.

4 Gradually lower the first two skeins into the dye bath, making sure that there is enough liquid in the pan for the wool to swim freely. Bring the pan to a simmer and keep it there for 60 minutes. During this processing hour, move the wool around occasionally, and very gently. Do not over-agitate or push it to the bottom of the pan: this is too hot for the wool and may scorch it, while over-agitation may felt it.

5 After processing, don your rubber gloves to remove the skeins. Good-quality gloves are heat-resistant so will allow you to handle very hot wool for short periods. They will also prevent accidental scalds and protect your hands from dye stains. Gently squeeze any excess liquid back into the dye bath, then place the wool in the colander to cool.

COLOURS FROM ONION SKINS

6 Remove the next two skeins from the second pan and lower them into the dye bath. Process these as for the first two.

7 Allow your wool to cool to the temperature of your warm tap water, then rinse the first two skeins in this until the rinsing water remains clear. Dissolve 1tbsp salt in the water for the last rinse; this will help to fix the dye.

8 Remove the skeins, gently squeeze out the excess water, then set them aside until all your dyeing is complete.

9 Repeat steps 4–8 for the last two skeins, then discard the remaining dye.

ONION SKIN: FIRST BATH

Second bath

Mordants: alum, chrome
Assistants: cream
of tartar, salt

ONION SKIN: SECOND BATH

1 Pour the second third
of your dye liquid into the
dye bath and top up to two-
thirds full with cold water.

2 Dissolve 30g (1oz) of
alum in a small amount of
boiling water and add to
the dye bath.

3 Lower the first two
skeins into the bath,
heating the wool first if
necessary, and process for
45 minutes.

4 As for the first bath,
begin to heat the four
remaining skeins in a
separate pan.

5 Ten minutes before
the end of the processing,
dissolve a small pinch of
chrome in a little hot
water. Lift the wool clear
of the dye bath with one
hand, pour in the chrome
with the other, then add a
pinch of cream of tartar.
Lower the wool back into
the dye bath and process
for a further 10 minutes.

6 Rinse the wool as for
the first onion dye bath
(see first bath, step 7).

7 Follow the procedure
in steps 5 and 6 for the
second and third dips.

8 Discard the remaining
dye and thoroughly clean
the pan to remove any
trace of chrome.

Third bath

Mordants: alum, tin
Assistants: salt

1 Set up the third onion
dye bath and proceed as for
the second, but add tin
instead of chrome.

2 When you have
finished, clean the dye pan
thoroughly with bleach,
then rinse well. Wash any
other vessels you have used
and clean up the
surrounding area.

ONION SKIN: THIRD BATH

SESSION TWO | COCHINEAL

You will only be dyeing for two colours in this session, but there will be more successive exhaust dips than for the onion dye, so you will need more skeins of wool – at least 20.

First bath

Mordants: alum, tin
Assistants: vinegar, salt

1 Place the soaked cochineal in a large pan with 1l of water (approx. 2pt), and simmer for 45 minutes.

2 Strain out the debris and return half the liquid to the dye pan.

3 Top up the pan with cold water. Dissolve 30g (1oz) of alum in a little boiling water and add this and 1tbsp of vinegar to the water. Stir well.

4 Immerse two skeins in the dye bath and a further eight in a second pan of water. Bring both pans to a simmer. Keep the dye pan simmering for 40 minutes. The wool in the second pan must be kept at the same temperature as the dye bath

until all the skeins have been removed for dyeing.

5 Dissolve a very small pinch of tin in 1tbsp of hot water, lift the wool clear of the dye bath while you add this, stir well then re-immerse the wool. Simmer for a further 15 minutes.

6 Remove the wool, squeeze out the excess liquid, then place the wool in a colander to cool.

7 Remove the next two skeins from the second pan and lower them gently into the dye bath.

8 Rinse the wool from the first dip in fresh water until the water runs clear. Add 1tbsp of salt to the final rinse.

9 Repeat steps 4–8 until the dye bath is exhausted (i.e., there is no further colour) or you have as many shades as you require.

10 Wash and clean the dye pan thoroughly.

COCHINEAL: FIRST BATH

Second bath

Mordants: alum, tin
Assistants: cream of tartar, salt

1 Place the remaining cochineal solution in your dye bath. Add 30g (1oz) of alum and 5g (⅛tsp) of cream of tartar. The dye bath should immediately

become a rich red; if not, add a second 5g (⅛tsp) of cream of tartar.

2 Follow the directions for the first cochineal dye bath, but omit the vinegar.

3 Clean your dye pan thoroughly with bleach and rinse well.

COCHINEAL: SECOND BATH

COLOURS FROM COCHINEAL

SESSION THREE | BRAZIL WOOD

In this session you will use your brazil wood dye to produce three colours, for which you will need 18 skeins of wool.

First bath

Mordant: alum
Assistant: salt

1 Place the contents of the brazil wood jar in your dye pan. Add 1.5l (3pt) of cold water, bring to a simmer and process for 90 minutes.

2 Strain out the debris and pour the liquid, in equal parts, into three separate jugs. Pour one-third back into the dye bath and top up with cold water so that the pan is two-thirds full.

BRAZIL WOOD: FIRST BATH

3 Dissolve 30g (1oz) of alum in a little boiling water, add to the dye pan and stir well.

4 Immerse two skeins of wool in the dye bath, bring to a simmer and process for 60 minutes.

5 In a second pan of water, begin to heat a further four skeins of wool.

6 Once your 60 minutes' processing has passed, remove the first two skeins, place them in your colander to cool, and gently immerse the second two skeins in your dye bath.

7 Continue as for the onion dye bath, following steps 7–9 of the first bath (see p 15).

Second bath

Mordants: alum, chrome
Assistant: salt

1 Pour another third of your brazil wood liquid into the dye pan.

2 Dissolve 30g (1oz) of alum in a little boiling water and add this to the dye pan.

3 Fill two-thirds of the pan with cold water, add the first two skeins of wool, bring to a simmer and process for 45 minutes.

4 Heat the remaining four skeins to the same temperature as the dye bath in a second pan.

BRAZIL WOOD: SECOND BATH

5 Once the processing time has elapsed, dissolve a pinch of chrome in a little hot water. Lift the wool clear of the dye bath briefly to stir in the chrome solution, then re-immerse the wool and process for a further 15 minutes.

6 Remove the wool and place it in your colander to cool.

7 Immerse the second two skeins in the dye bath.

8 Rinse the first two skeins as for the onion-skin dye, remembering to add salt to the final rinse.

9 Follow the same procedure until all your skeins for this bath have been processed.

Third bath
Mordants: alum, copper
Assistant: salt

Follow the directions as for the second brazil wood bath, but this time substitute copper for chrome.

BRAZIL WOOD: THIRD BATH

COLOURS FROM BRAZIL WOOD

SESSION FOUR | DYER'S-WEED (BROOM)

With this dye you will be making only two dye baths; the dye liquid will be split into three as usual but one-third will be saved for mixing with the logwood, in session 5.

First bath
Mordant: alum
Assistant: salt

DYER'S-WEED: FIRST BATH

COLOURS FROM DYER'S-WEED

1 Add the contents of your dyer's-weed jar to your pan, cover with water and simmer for 60 minutes.

2 Strain out the debris from the dye liquid and pour the liquid into three separate jugs. Now pour one-third back into the jar, one-third into the dye pan and the remaining third, for the second dye bath, into a jug.

3 Follow the same procedure as for the first onion dye bath (see p 15).

Second bath
Mordants: alum, copper
Assistant: salt

Follow the same procedure as for the first bath but add a pinch of copper 15 minutes before the end of the processing time and return to a simmer.

DYER'S-WEED: SECOND BATH

MADDER: SECOND BATH

SESSION FIVE | MADDER

You will only be producing two colours with your madder, but you may need more wool than usual; you can never get enough of the wonderful reds it produces, so it is well worth using every single drop.

First bath
Mordant: alum
Assistants: chalk, salt

1 Rinse the madder in a sieve, ensuring that the granules don't pass through the holes.

2 Place this rinsed madder in your dye pan, cover with cold water and bring to a slow simmer. Do not allow to boil: boiling destroys alizarin, the element that produces the red, and produces vile yellows instead. Simmer for 90 minutes.

3 Pour the liquid off into a large clean container (such as a washing-up bowl), leaving the madder in the dye pan.

4 Cover the reserved madder with water, bring to a simmer and process for another 90 minutes.

5 Repeat steps 3 and 4.

6 This time strain off the madder and return the liquid to the dye bath. Keep the first three pourings for the second dye bath.

7 Fill two-thirds of the pan with cold water. Dissolve 30g (1oz) of alum and ½tsp of powdered chalk in a little boiling water and add this to the dye bath. (If you have no chalk, talcum powder has the same effect.)

8 Immerse the first two skeins in the dye bath and process for 90 minutes. Remember, it is very important that the madder dye bath does not boil.

9 As before, have a second dye pan heating the remaining wool.

10 Continue to process the wool in the same way as for the earlier dye lots.

Second bath
Mordants: alum, tin
Assistants: cream of tartar, salt

1 Return the liquid poured from the initial simmering (steps 2–5 of the first bath) to the dye bath.

2 Dissolve 30g (1oz) of alum and ½tsp of cream of tartar in a little boiling water and add this to the dye bath.

3 Process your skeins in the same way as the first madder bath but add a pinch of tin dissolved in hot water 15 minutes before the end, then replace the wool and continue to simmer for the remaining processing time.

4 Continue with exhaust dips until you have enough dyed wool or until the bath is exhausted of colour.

COLOURS FROM MADDER

MADDER: FIRST BATH

SESSION SIX | LOGWOOD

This session, which uses the last batch of your dyer's-weed liquid, will produce four colours. Again, you will need 18 skeins.

COLOURS FROM LOGWOOD

First bath

Mordant: alum
Assistant: salt

Follow the same procedure as for the first onion-skin bath (see p 15), but simmer the logwood for 90 minutes.

LOGWOOD: FIRST BATH

Second bath

Mordants: alum, iron
Assistant: salt

Add the second third of logwood liquid to the dye bath along with 30g (1oz) of alum. This time bloom 15 minutes from the end with a good pinch of iron, then proceed as for the onion-skin dye bath.

Third bath

Mordants: alum, copper
Assistant: salt
Additional dyestuff: dyer's-weed

1 Place the remaining logwood liquid and the last of the dyer's-weed liquid in the same dye pan. Add 30g (1oz) of alum and the first two skeins of wool, bring to a simmer and process for 45 minutes.

2 Heat the remaining skeins in a second pan.

3 After the 45 minutes' processing, add a good pinch of copper to the first two skeins and process for a further 15 minutes.

4 Continue as for the other onion-skin dye bath.

LOGWOOD: THIRD BATH

LOGWOOD: SECOND BATH

Surface decoration using dyes and paints

People have been decorating fabrics for as long as they have been making them. The ancient Egyptians extracted dyes from plants and used them to dye and paint fabrics. Dyes and paints also have a long history in India; tie-dyed fabrics and elaborately painted chintzes dating back over 2,000 years, and printing blocks dating back to 3000BC have been discovered.

In China and Japan fabric decoration was taken to a high degree of skill. The Chinese developed the technique of cutting elaborate designs into paper and applying colour through them. Sometimes dozens of stencils were used in one design, each stencil forming a different element of it. This was the beginnings of screen printing.

As the fabric used to decorate dolls' houses and dress miniature dolls is likely to be washed only very rarely, if at all, a whole new world of colour application is opened up. Any medium can be used to decorate the fabrics, including glued-on designs using flock, glitter and beads. While there are some specialist glues that will stand up to laundering, even those recommend dry-cleaning.

One of the main considerations with fabrics used in miniatures is the handling of the material after any decoration has been applied. The fabric must remain soft enough to drape, although this is not as important in fabrics to be used for upholstery that will be stretched and held in place. Also important is to match the nature of the colouring agent with the fabric, for example, a dye made with acrylic paint (as is commonly used in screen printing) will remain matt in the surface of the fabric, defeating the whole purpose of using a fabric with a sheen such as silk. Dyes work in one of two basic ways:

❦ they penetrate the fibres of the fabric

❦ they stick to the surface of the fibres

The main difference between these processes is that penetrating dyes leave the handle of the fabric unchanged, making them suitable for use with clothing and other articles that are required to drape. Dyes and paints that remain on the surface of the fabric, making them a little stiffer, are more suitable for use on fabrics to be used for upholstery.

SILK PAINTS, DYE PENS AND WATER-SOLUBLE GUTTA WERE USED TO CREATE THIS DESIGN

PREPARING THE FABRIC

Most fabrics leave the manufacturer with a finish on them, unless they are specifically prepared for dyeing. They may contain wax, starch, oil, dirt or size (a gelatinous mixture used to seal fabrics and paper). Unless removed, these contaminants can lead to an uneven take-up of the dye and prevent a good bond between the dye and the fabric. Wash, dry and iron your fabric at the appropriate temperature. Stretch and pin the fabric to a suitable frame. This could be a silk-painting frame, a picture frame, an embroidery hoop – anything so long as the fabric is taught and evenly stretched. An embroidery hoop is the most suitable for small projects if you need to stretch something quickly, and you don't need to pin the fabric to hold it in place. Now you are ready to get creative.

COLOUR APPLICATION

There are several very simple methods of applying colourful decoration to fabrics. Dye pens, paints and wax crayons can all be used to great effect.

Dye pens

Dye pens look like thick felt-tip pens but have a surprisingly fine point for their size. Their colours are bright and strong and, after fixing, permanent. Their one drawback is that they have a tendency to bleed on fine fabrics, which can be a problem with miniature work. For this reason they are sometimes used with a resist (see p 31). They can be used in the same way as conventional felt-tip pens or rested on the surface of the fabric to allow the dye to flow into it.

ALTHOUGH THE CASINGS ARE THICK, DYE PENS HAVE A FINE POINT

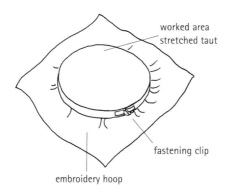

worked area stretched taut

fastening clip

embroidery hoop

STRETCH THE FABRIC WHEN YOU MOUNT IT IN A FRAME OR HOOP

Move the pen slowly over the area to be coloured until you have reached the depth of colour required or the fabric is saturated. To fix the colour, iron the fabric at the appropriate temperature for between two and five minutes. The length of time depends on the pens used; instructions will come with the pens or be available from the supplier. Some dye pens do not require fixing beyond being allowed to dry thoroughly.

Home-made dye pens

Buying a large range of dye pens can be expensive. If you have powder dyes in the primary colours and a handful of empty cake-icing pens, it is possible to make your own large selection of dye pens. It is even possible to charge the pens with silk paints.

The main advantage of using cake-icing pens is that they have a very fine point, which is ideal for miniatures. Since the pens are supplied with three wicks you can use each pen for three colours, providing the point is first bleached free of the previous dye. If you are using silk paints in the pens, just pop a wick into the jar of paint, remove it when it is charged, then position it in the icing pen. If you are using dyes, stand the wick in a small jar of the dye solution; the dye will be drawn up into the wick.

Silk paints can be mixed to produce new colours – any other dye type should be made up according to the manufacturer's instructions, with a fixative added if necessary. It is worth bearing in mind that you will only need about 10ml (2tsp) of dye for each pen; it might be a good idea to do a little arithmetic, to save having to store any excess dye. However, if you are intending to use a lot of one colour it would be better to make up more, as you won't be able to match the colour if you run out. Make up 50ml (2fl oz) of each primary colour, plus black and white, and use 40ml (1½fl oz) of each for mixing to obtain secondary and tertiary colours.

If your dye pens are proving stubborn in starting, try standing the point in a little of the dye solution. For both silk paints and acrylic pigments, fix the colour with a dry iron. You should iron directly onto the fabric; cover it, with a clean sheet of paper, only if the fabric is delicate.

CAKE ICING PENS CAN BE FILLED WITH FABRIC DYE

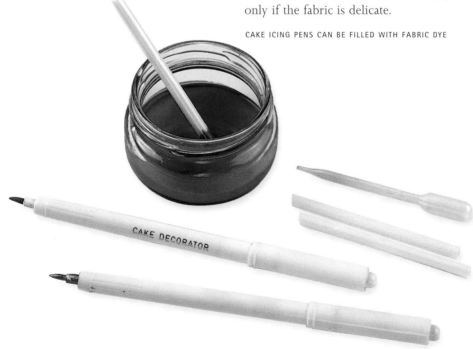

Dye paints

Dye paints work in a similar way to dye pens except that they can be used directly from the jar and applied by brush or sponge, or thinned and applied by spray gun or in any other conceivable way. Dye paints can be used on their own, free flowing, or added to a fabric medium.

Free-flowing dyes should be used only if you want the dye to spread or in conjunction with a resist or gutta. Because such dyes penetrate the fibres of the fabric, they leave its handle unchanged. Thickened dyes should be used if you don't want to use a resist or gutta, and for screen printing: you cannot use free-flowing dyes for screen printing as they would pour through the mesh all in one place. Because they won't spread, it is possible to achieve very fine detail with thickened dyes. Unless you are very skilled with resists and guttas, such detail isn't possible with free-flowing paints. Thickened dyes tend to stay mostly on the surface of a fabric, though some penetration will occur. If you want an acrylic dye to be permanent, it must be added to a fabric medium.

If you want to paint directly onto the fabric without using a resist, or if you want to add fine detail to an already coloured design, you can thicken silk paints and made-up dye powders with a proprietary thickener, such as Manutex, or by adding wallpaper paste; vegans should be aware

DYE PAINTS CAN BE USED THICKENED, THINNED OR STRAIGHT FROM THE TUBE

SAMPLES DECORATED WITH TRANSFER INKS

that wallpaper paste contains animal by-products. (If you don't want to use animal products, use a starch-based resist made from corn or wheat flour [see p 31]). It takes only a little wallpaper paste to thicken a liquid dye, so start with a very small amount (for instance, ½tsp of paste to 50ml (2fl oz) of dye liquid). Remember, you cannot take any out if you add too much, so be sparing in the first place.

The dye paint should be made just thick enough to stay where you put it, so have handy a small piece of fabric on which to test its viscosity. Watch your test piece for a few minutes to make sure there is no delayed bleed, then dry iron it, wash it with a mild soap, and iron again to dry. Having thus subjected the test piece to heat, water, soap and steam you will be able to tell whether the colour will stay where you want it and whether the paint consistency is right.

Although acrylic paints will not penetrate the fabric fibres fully like a dye, providing they are not applied too heavily, the fabric will remain quite soft.

Both silk paints and acrylic pigments should be fixed with a dry iron.

ACRYLIC PAINTS SUCH AS THESE SHOULD BE FIXED
WITH A DRY IRON

FABRIC MEDIUMS CAN BE USED TO THICKEN
ACRYLIC PAINTS

TRANSFER PAINTS REQUIRE THE HEAT FROM AN IRON TO
MOVE THE COLOUR FROM THE STENCIL TO THE FABRIC

DYE POWDERS CAN BE MIXED TO PRODUCE UNLIMITED COLOURS, AND USED IN CAKE-ICING PENS

Silk paints

I tend to use silk paints because of their versatility. They are usually bought as semi-fluid liquids which can be diluted with water to make them free flowing or thickened further and used without a resist or gutta. They are easy to fix, colour-fast, and are available in a huge range of colours and special finishes, such as pearl and metallic. Silk paints are commonly used with a resist as they will bleed unless thickened. (See the cushion panels on p 32 for samples.)

A SAMPLE PAINTED WITH DILUTED SILK PAINTS

IT IS OFTEN HARD TO TELL WHAT COLOUR A POWDER WILL PRODUCE AS MANY ARE VERY DARK IN THIS FORM; THIS POWDER GIVES A BRIGHT BLUE

SILK PAINTS ARE PARTICULARLY VERSATILE

THIS ACID DYE WAS PRODUCED BY ADDING AN ACIDIC LIQUID TO A RED DYE POWDER

NIBS OF DIFFERENT WIDTHS ARE AVAILABLE FOR USE WITH TUBES OF PAINT

Bowls × 2, 1 heatproof
Wooden spoon
Saucepan
Plain white flour, 50g (2oz)
Cold water, 50ml (2fl oz)
Gum arabic solution, 50ml (2fl oz) (available from art shops)

BATIK WAX IS AN EFFECTIVE
RESIST BUT QUITE TIME-
CONSUMING TO REMOVE

ACROBATIK CAN BE USED FOR
STENCILLING, BLOCK PRINTING,
TIE DYEING AND SPONGING

Resists

A resist is a substance that is painted onto fabric in order to prevent a dye or paint from spreading into areas where you do not want it.

There are several commercial products that can be used as resists. These include wax (as used in batik), gutta (used for silk painting), and proprietary products such as Dylon's Acrobatik. The main thing to consider when choosing which to use is how readily they can be removed. Some resists cannot be removed. Wax requires lengthy ironing on an absorbent surface. Gutta is a little more friendly; solvent-based guttas can be removed by dry cleaning and water-based guttas will wash out. Some carry a pigment that will remain behind when the gutta has been removed – this is useful if you plan to outline a design. I have yet to discover a method of removal for Acrobatik.

In my opinion our ancestors had the best method of blocking areas; they used a starch-based resist. I have used the recipe below successfully with all types of dye products. Don't make up more than you'll need: it will keep for a few weeks at the most, after which it becomes difficult to remove from the fabric.

Starch-based resist

The amounts given will make 150ml (5fl oz). Processing time is five minutes.

1 In a heatproof bowl, gradually add the water to the flour and stir until it forms a smooth paste.

2 Place the bowl in a saucepan and carefully pour a little hot water into the pan; just enough to come a quarter of the way up the sides of the bowl.

3 Stir the mixture over a medium heat until it thickens. It will change a little in colour as it cooks.

4 Remove from the heat source, pour the contents out of the saucepan into a clean bowl, and allow to cool a little.

5 Stir the gum arabic in briskly, a little at a time. If the mixture is still too thick – it should have the consistency of double cream – add a little more water.

6 If there are any lumps, strain the mixture through a sieve to remove them. For best results, store in an airtight jar and use within two weeks.

BOTH CLEAR AND COLOURED GUTTAS ARE AVAILABLE

31

ACRYLIC PAINTS THICKEND WITH FABRIC
MEDIUM WERE USED WITH NO RESIST

CUSHION DESIGN PAINTED USING A STARCH-
BASED RESIST AND SILK PAINTS

DESIGN PAINTED USING WATER-SOLUBLE
GUTTA WITH GOLD PIGMENT ADDED, SILK
PAINTS AND DYE PENS

FOR THIS DESIGN I USED SILK PAINT
THICKENED WITH WALLPAPER PASTE, AND
NO RESIST

DESIGN FOR MOTTLED BLUE CUSHION

DESIGN FOR GREEN CUSHION

I USED ACRYLIC PAINTS THICKENED WITH
FABRIC MEDIUM TO DECORATE THIS BED
LINEN, ALONG WITH A STARCH-BASED RESIST

DESIGN FOR SUNFLOWER CUSHION   DESIGN FOR CREAM CUSHION

DESIGN FOR
PAINTED BED
VALANCE   DESIGN FOR BED COVERLET

DESIGN FOR PAINTED BED CURTAINS, LEFT AND RIGHT

Wax fabric crayons

With fabric crayons all the work is done on paper, then transferred to the fabric using the heat of an iron. The colours will change slightly on being transferred, so it is wise to test each colour before embarking on a project.

The two most commonly available wax fabric crayons are Dylon and Crayola. Crayola crayons are the perfect width for sharpening in a pencil sharpener; Dylon crayons can be sharpened with a craft knife or large pencil sharpener. Blending the crayons on paper can give you some interesting results.

Compressed paper sticks are sold in art and craft shops for this purpose. A heavier application on the paper will result in a deeper colour on the fabric. This is very useful when working with a limited palette; paler shades can be obtained simply through a lighter application. Use a good-quality thin paper.

Draw, trace or photocopy your design and colour it in. Embroidery designs are a good source of pictures, but be aware that you cannot use them for commercial purposes. If you can find any small enough, colour an embroidery transfer and iron this onto your fabric. Such transfers can be used repeatedly until the colour and the transfer become too faint.

SAMPLE DESIGNS COLOURED WITH
WAX FABRIC CRAYONS

DESIGN FOR WAX CRAYON PAINTING

ALTERNATIVE DESIGN FOR WAX CRAYON PAINTING

Children's wax crayons

I don't think I'd handled wax crayons since my childhood – until I discovered this new use for them. I tend to use them for designs that are big and bold. It will work on both cotton and silk. On cotton it produces an effect similar to chintz, with the wax contributing a glazed appearance to the finished design.

The colours do tend to bleed a little on cotton; using gutta to outline a design will help overcome this. Outlining in this way can also be used to simulate batik. On the Fauve-style silk sample (see p 41), the bleeding is hardly noticeable; it simply gives a soft finish. The coloured fabric can be washed in warm water with mild soap.

CHILDREN'S WAX CRAYONS CAN BE USED ON FABRICS

37

Tin cans for each colour, well
washed and thoroughly dried

Saucepan

Rubber gloves

Clingfilm

Scales

Stirrer (the handle of an
old spoon or a clean
wooden stick will do)

Pencil sharpener

Small tins of fibre-reactive,
cold-water dye, in colours
of your choice

Batik wax (ordinary candle
wax is unsuitable; the wax
must contain beeswax)

Paper

Home-made wax crayons

1 Line the scales and cover your working areas with clingfilm to prevent them from being contaminated.

2 Weigh the contents of one or more tins of dye powder, then set aside. One tin will make one fat crayon or three thin ones. Place an equal weight of batik wax in the empty tin.

3 Place this tin in the saucepan and pour a little hot water carefully into the pan – enough to cover the bottom of the pan but not so much that the can floats. Do not get any water in the wax: water in hot wax will cause it to spit and explode and it will burn if it lands on your skin.

4 Place the pan on the hob and melt the wax over a medium heat.

5 As soon as the wax liquifies, remove the pan from the heat and the tin from the saucepan. Pour the dye powder into the tin and stir thoroughly. Pour this mixture carefully onto your film-covered work area. As it cools, form the coloured wax into a ball and manipulate it until it is nice and smooth. Finally, roll it into a stick, about the width of a pencil, before it hardens. The warmth from your hands should keep the wax pliable until it is rolled out. Do not wear rubber gloves while manipulating: the wax will stick to them.

6 Set the crayon aside to cool and sharpen with a pencil sharpener when the wax is hard. Wrap a band of paper around the crayon and write the dye number on it (this will be written on the tin) so you can repeat the colour whenever you wish.

7 Use as you would any other dye crayon. The dye stick will not stain your hands, providing they are not soaking wet.

MY HOME-MADE WAX CRAYONS

Printing with stamps

There are some very good miniature stamps available from craft shops and mail-order suppliers. You can also have stamps made up from your own drawings – if they are clear enough – and the results are very good. Companies that provide this service are listed in the advertisement sections of arts and craft magazines.

The small, coloured ink pads sold along with stamps give very good, sharp results. The inks can be fixed with a dry iron. For more permanent, completely colourfast results, dye pens and crayons can be used; rub the colour onto a surface such as a ceramic tile, and the tile will act as a dye pad.

SAMPLE DESIGN CREATED WITH MINIATURE STAMPS

MINIATURE STAMPS ARE READILY AVAILABLE AND EASY TO USE

USING WAX FABRIC CRAYONS

1 Transfer your chosen pattern to the fabric by tracing with an embroidery pencil, using a small iron on an embroidery transfer, or by drawing freehand.

2 Place a sheet of clean paper under the fabric and your coloured design face-down on top of the fabric.

3 With your iron set to cotton, apply heat to the design for one minute; do not move the iron about or you risk blurring the image.

4 Hold the design firmly in place and lift one corner to check the depth of colour. If the transfer is too pale, apply the iron for a further minute.

5 If you wish to define the pattern, outline the design with a ballpoint pen.

USING A WARM IRON TO TRANSFER
A WAX CRAYON DESIGN

paper with coloured design

clean paper   fabric

USING CHILDREN'S WAX CRAYONS

EQUIPMENT
AND MATERIALS

Iron

Children's wax crayons

Blotting paper × 2 sheets

Fabric

Suitable design

1 Place the fabric on top of a sheet of blotting paper, on a heatproof surface. Set the iron to a moderate temperature, then heat the fabric and blotting paper just enough to soften the wax when you press a crayon to it. This should only take a few seconds. Begin colouring in the design straight away, keeping the paper under the fabric warm, but not too hot, as you work. If the paper is too hot, the wax will melt as soon as the crayon touches the fabric, making it difficult to spread the colour. Don't be too heavy handed with the colours: a light touch gives a better result, and you won't have so much wax to iron out afterwards.

2 Cover the fabric with the second sheet of blotting paper and press with a warm iron: this will help remove the excess wax and set the colours.

FAUVE-STYLE SAMPLES COLOURED
WITH CHILDREN'S WAX CRAYONS

Devoré velvet

The word devoré comes from the French 'dévorer', meaning to devour. Devoré solution can be used to great effect in creating miniature etched velvet. I use it to make the cut-pile velvet that was so popular during the Elizabethan era (mid- to late sixteenth century) and typical of the Victorian Gothic style (mid-nineteenth century). The velvets used in these times were not produced by chemical means but by laboriously cutting the pile with a very sharp blade. The devoré solution only reacts with silk-and-viscose velvet (i.e. velvet that has a viscose pile and a silk backing). It works by producing an acid that, when heated, burns away the pile to which it has been applied. Also known as Fibre Etch, this solution is available from mail-order suppliers and craft stores. There are several solutions available for use on different types of fabric.

DEVORE PASTE

FIBRE ETCH

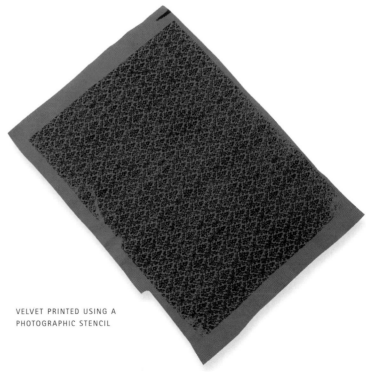

VELVET PRINTED USING A
PHOTOGRAPHIC STENCIL

SCREEN PRINTING

Devoré solution can be applied with a brush but for a more controlled and finely detailed finish, it is best applied by screen printing. This is far less daunting than it first appears; screen printing is just another form of stencilling. The screen is basically a wooden frame with a fine silk or mesh stretched over it. You apply the stencil to the mesh and force the solution or thickened dye through the gaps and onto the fabric below.

You can either purchase a ready-made frame, with the fabric already stretched onto it, or make your own. The frame must be very strong and the screen fabric must be stretched extremely tightly across it. This task is usually performed by a special machine; with home-made screens, the fabric may relax and become a little loose when it is wet. To combat this, wet the fabric before fixing it to the frame, then stretch and staple it into position, stretching and placing as much tension on the fabric as you possibly can. This is much easier with silk than with synthetic, purpose-made screen meshes. For printing miniature fabric, the screen must be not less than 30 × 35cm (12 × 14in). The fabric may be ordinary fine, lightweight silk or the fine mesh made expressly for screen printing.

MY WELL-USED SCREEN-PRINTING FRAME

PREPARING THE STENCIL

There are several methods and materials that can be used for making screen-printing stencils. Whichever method you choose, seal the join between the screen fabric and the frame inside the recess with gummed paper tape, right up to the edges of the design. This paper tape will prevent any dye paste or devoré solution from creeping past the blocked-out areas.

Paper stencils

This method uses a sheet of paper to make a negative image. Cut your design from the sheet, using a craft knife or scissors, then tape the cut-out to the underside – the flat side – of the screen. Whether you are using thickened dye or devoré, the paper will stick to the screen after the first pass of the squeegee.

It is not worth the effort of working in too much detail as a screen of this type cannot be used more than two or three times; after this the dye or devoré will begin to penetrate the paper, colouring areas that are not part of the design. The stencil will eventually develop holes and tear. However, you can extend the life of a paper stencil by coating it with vegetable oil or shellac. Allow this to dry before fixing the stencil to the screen.

Remember to leave 'bridges' (i.e. links of paper) on the stencil in strategic places to prevent areas from falling out before you can attach it to the screen. This requires some thought and forward planning. Be careful not to get any glue on the bridges when you are sticking it in place. Once the design has adhered, remove the bridges.

design motif

bridge

SOME DESIGNS NEED PAPER BRIDGES TO HOLD THEM TOGETHER

THE EASIEST WAY TO APPLY YOUR PAINT OR DYE IS TO USE A SQUEEGEE

Painted stencils

This technique uses shellac or a purpose-made filling solution to block up holes in the mesh in order to create either a negative or a positive image. A shellac stencil will not give very fine detail in the printing; a filling agent will give much more detail because it is less inclined to bleed into the surrounding fabric.

If you paint in, and thus block, the negative parts of the design (i.e. the background), a positive image will be printed onto the velvet, while if you block the positive parts, the screen will only print the background.

It is very important to hold the screen up to a window or a light source to check for pinholes in the blocked-out areas. Small holes in the blocking will allow dye or devoré to penetrate and colour areas that you want left blank. A painted stencil does take some time to make.

A shellac-coated stencil will not last as long as one that has been made with a filling agent. Shellac reacts with alcohol-based dyes and degrades with repeated use. If you check regularly for pin-size holes and touch up any you find with shellac, a stencil could last from 20 to 30 strike-offs (printings).

A proprietary filling agent will last almost indefinitely; I don't think I have ever worn out a screen made with this.

To make a stencilled screen using this method, place your design template centrally on the inside recessed area of the screen, tape it in position and paint over the design with the shellac or filling solution, on the underside of the screen. Be sure to remove the template before the blocking agent dries or it will stick.

Profilm stencils

Profilm is a paper coated with a layer of lacquer; profilm stencils can be used to make a positive or a negative image; if you cut away the design you will print a positive image, if you cut away the background you will print a negative image.

Place your design under a profilm sheet with the lacquer side facing up. Using a very sharp knife, trace the design to score the lacquer – the lacquer only – and peel it away from the backing sheet, which should be left intact. Cut away only the positive image.

Place the sheet centrally on the underside of the screen, then cover the inside recessed area with greaseproof paper. Press the stencil by moving a warm iron slowly over it until the lacquer sticks to the screen. Allow it to cool before removing the backing sheet and greaseproof paper.

This type of screen has the same limitations as painted stencils using shellac, though they will last a little longer. It takes a bit of practice to cut the lacquer without cutting the backing but it is possible, if a bit tedious, to get a finely detailed stencil.

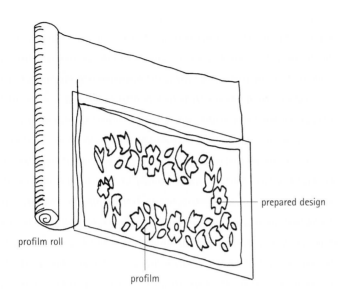

prepared design

profilm roll

profilm

STEP 1: CUT THE PROFILM TO SIZE

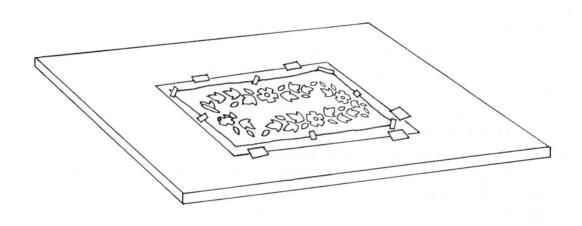

STEP 2: TAPE YOUR DESIGN TO A FLAT SURFACE, THEN TAPE THE PROFILM OVER YOUR DESIGN

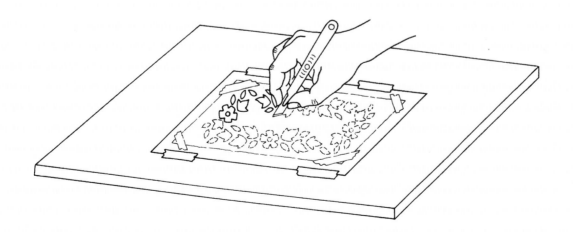

STEP 3: SCORE THE DESIGN USING JUST ENOUGH PRESSURE TO SCORE THE LACQUER, BUT NOT THE BACKING

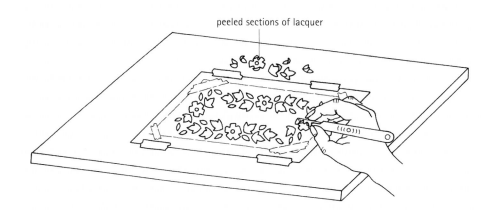

peeled sections of lacquer

STEP 4: PEEL AWAY THE SCORED
LACQUER LAYER OF THE PROFILM

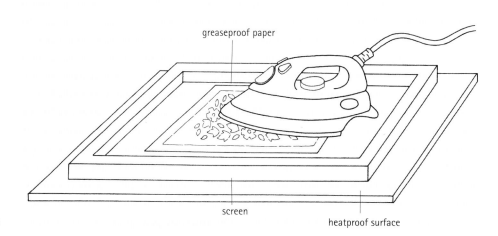

greaseproof paper

screen

heatproof surface

STEP 5: PLACE THE DESIGN
LACQUER-SIDE UP ON A
HEATPROOF SURFACE AND CENTRE
THE SCREEN, RECESSED SIDE UP,
OVER THE DESIGN. COVER THE
DESIGN WITH GREASEPROOF PAPER
AND PRESS WITH A WARM IRON

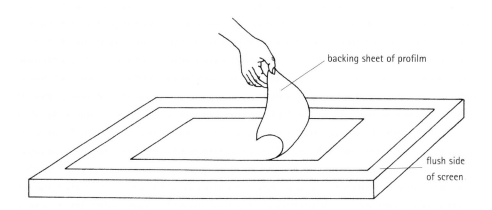

backing sheet of profilm

flush side
of screen

STEP 6: WHEN COLD, TURN THE
SCREEN OVER, PEEL OFF THE
BACKING SHEET, COAT ALL AREAS
OUTSIDE THE DESIGN WITH
SHELLAC, THEN REMOVE THE
GREASEPROOF PAPER

Photographic stencils

A photographically produced stencil will give the finest detail imaginable and will last almost indefinitely. If you intend to print a lot of fabric, this should be your method of choice. The stencil can be produced in a screen-printing studio from your own positive drawing, or you can make one yourself.

A product called Speedball will allow you to produce a photographic stencil without using a darkroom. Speedball is developed using a 150W light bulb, so the stencil can be prepared using low or ordinary room light. Speedball screen preparation is sold in kit form by good art stores and comes with full instructions. I have found it simple to use and very durable. I have also had several stencils made at a friendly art college. As they are able to use large vacuum compression machines, dark rooms and spray-cleaning tanks, the image they produce is as pristine as the original artwork.

Draw your artwork for photographic stencils with the blackest ink pen you can find. Photocopy it onto acetate, then touch it up with ink to ensure that no light can penetrate the drawn areas. This is very important: the acetate copy will be used to transfer the design to the screen and any light penetration in the wrong place will adversely affect the clarity of your final print.

Mix the photograph emulsion and sensitizer together in the recommended proportions, then spread this mixture onto both sides of the screen with a squeegee or a piece of stiff card. When the emulsion is dry, lay a sheet of clean white paper on the inside of the screen, and top this with a block of sponge or a thick pad of newspapers.

Turn the screen over, place your positive acetate image centrally on the screen and cover it with a sheet of clean glass to ensure that the acetate is in full contact with the screen. Now it is time to expose your template to the light source for the required period of time. After this, wash the screen. Where the blocking agent was exposed to the light it will have hardened, while the unexposed areas (those under the drawing ink) will have remained soft; only the soft areas will wash away. Always hold the screen up to the light to make sure that the emulsion has been removed from all the design lines; use a small, soft nailbrush to remove any remaining sections. It is also a good idea to check for any areas that should have been blocked out that aren't; these should be touched up with screen filler.

AN EMULSION KIT CONSISTS OF
TWO SEPARATE LIQUIDS

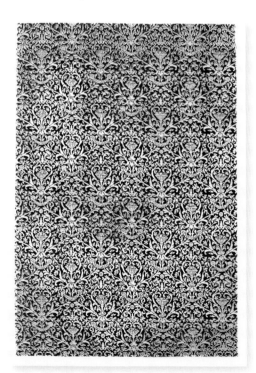

A PHOTOGRAPHIC STENCIL

CREATING DEVORE VELVET

Before you begin, make sure you are working in a well-ventilated area. The fumes given off when the burn-out phase is reached can be quite acrid, so wear a mask and eye protection.

ON DARK COLOURS, DEVORE
PATTERNS CAN BE VERY SUBTLE

Prepared screen

Squeegee (must be wider than the design area but narrower than the screen recess)

Spoon (must be large enough to dollop the solution onto the screen)

Old bed sheet or large piece of waste fabric

Pins

Iron

Dust mask

Devoré solution (must have the consistency of smooth double cream; if it doesn't, thin the solution with a little water)

Newspapers

Large sheet of white paper or wallpaper lining paper

Silk-and-viscose velvet

Tin of cold-water dye or dye of your choice (the velvet is only supplied in white)

1 Cover your working area with a thick pad of clean newspapers, then cover these with a large sheet of white paper or lining paper. Be sure that the whole area under the screen is evenly covered, then add a final layer of old sheet or waste fabric. Pin the velvet to the sheet, pile-side up, and align the screen with the velvet.

2 Spoon half the devoré paste along the top of the screen, above the print area, evenly and in a line.

3 Cut this paste in half with the blade of the squeegee. Tilt the squeegee to an angle of 45° and pull it towards you while pressing down. It helps if you can have someone else hold down the screen while you do this.

4 Repeat with the other half of the paste.

5 Without moving the screen, go to the other end of the fabric and repeat steps 2, 3 and 4, with the remainder of the solution.

6 Ease up the screen and remove the fabric, then set it aside until perfectly dry.

7 Iron the fabric at a high temperature, being careful not to scorch the untreated areas; if you prefer, place the fabric in an oven that has been preheated to 170°C (340°F) for five minutes. The treated areas will turn dark brown and carbonize.

8 Brush the fabric with your hands to remove the carbon, being careful not to tear it. When you have removed as much as possible, rinse the fabric in warm water and detergent. This should dislodge any remaining residue. Rinse well.

9 Dye the fabric at this point or for later dyeing.

10 Wash your screen well before any remaining devoré solution has time to dry on. Clean up your work area and vacuum to remove any carbon dust.

DEVORE VELVET CAN BE USED IN CLOTHING AND FOR UPHOLSTERY

Patchwork and quilting

It is likely that the beginnings of patchwork lie in the need to repair clothing, with a patch used to cover a hole. With the human desire to be creative, it is a very short step from a utilitarian to a decorative patch. Economy has been the driving factor for all the patchwork, quilting and appliqué forms we know so well today; our ancestors wasted nothing. Cheaper fabrics and pieces from worn-out clothing were used in patchwork to create bed furnishings. Patchwork and quilting are separate art forms; much patchwork is not quilted, and many quilted bed covers are made from uncut fabric. It is only in the last 150 years that the two forms have been coupled.

Using a computer and a printer it is easy to reproduce exact replicas of full-size fabrics in miniature. This technique is particularly useful for producing coverlets and quilts. A patchwork layered with wadding (batting) and a backing is called a coverlet; if the stitches are worked through all the layers it becomes a quilt.

QUILTING THREADS AND NEEDLES

My two threads of choice are Madeira tanne, No. 50 or Egyptian gassed cotton, No. 120. Madeira tanne is much easier to quilt with than gassed cotton, but there is no doubt that gassed cotton gives a superior finish, so it is worth persevering with. The trick is not to pull too hard, thread the needle with the end cut from the spool, and wax the thread to strengthen it and lessen the drag when you pull it through the fabric. The needles to use are size 12 quilting needles. These look very small, but if you always use the cut end of the thread or a fine needle-threader, they are easier to use than they look.

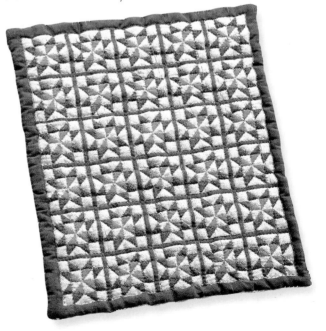

I CREATED THIS DESIGN USING A DRAWING PROGRAM ON MY COMPUTER

EQUIPMENT AND MATERIALS
Embroidery frame
Assa pins
Scissors
Iron
Voile (backing fabric)
Wadding
Cotton lawn
Appropriate design
Embroidery cotton

FRAMES

When making a full-size quilt a frame is essential in order to control the very large pieces of fabric and all the layers, but I tend not to use a frame when working at this scale: the problems of control don't arise with miniatures and in fact, when you're trying to keep your stitches small, a frame can be a hindrance. If you do use a frame you will need an embroidery or silk painting frame with an open area of not less than 12.5 × 15cm (5 × 6in).

Working with a frame

ASSA PINS

1 Start at the centre of each side, pinning the backing fabric from the centre out to the edges. Pin the top and one side first, then stretch the fabric to the other two sides.

2 Lay the wadding over the backing and trim to the dimensions of the inside of the frame.

3 Scan the quilt design or, using your saved design, print onto your previously prepared cotton lawn. Press with a hot iron.

4 Centre the design over the wadding and pin it to the top edge of the frame in the same manner as the backing. Do not over-stretch the fabric or the design will distort.

THE FABRICS AND DESIGN MOUNTED IN THE FRAME, READY FOR WORKING

Working without a frame

1 Place the three pieces of fabric together with the voile backing at the bottom, then the wadding and, finally, the printed lawn on top.

2 Tack through all of the layers diagonally with stitches of 2.5cm (1in). This is sufficient to hold everything in position until there is enough quilting in place to do the job.

3 Check regularly to make sure that your work is not distorting; if it is, pull it gently back into shape and continue.

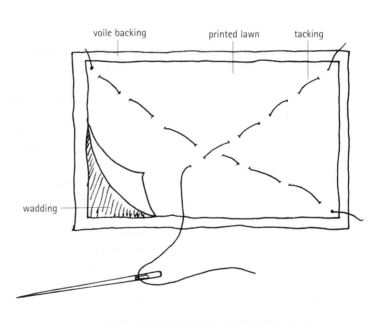

LAYERS OF FABRIC AND WADDING ARE HELD IN PLACE WITH ROWS OF TACKING

FABRICS

When using dyes and inks, it is always best to use natural fabrics, such as cotton, linen or silk: synthetic fibres, even if the fabric will accept the ink, alter the colours substantially. Try to suit the fabric to its final use. For instance, if you are printing a rug, it would look too even and smooth if you printed it on a fabric such as cotton lawn, so use a fabric with a pronounced weave.

Preparing the fabric

Wash and dry the fabric to remove any factory finish, iron at the recommended temperature, and set aside until required. Do not fold the fabric after ironing as any creases will cause problems for you when you stick it to the backing. As well as making it difficult to smooth the fabric onto the sticky surface of the page label, a crease will not allow the ink to penetrate, so the fabric underneath will remain unprinted.

THE COLOURS OF DYES AND INKS GIVE A MORE RELIABLE RESULT ON NATURAL FABRICS

PRINTING DESIGNS

Even computers can be incorporated into your miniatures hobby. You can print images directly onto your fabric, and create, touch-up or fill in patterns using drawing programs. Internet access is useful; most libraries have low-cost access and you can download graphics onto disk. Floppy disks have a limited storage capacity and graphics files can take up a lot of space; you may need to invest in a Zip drive. However, if the library has a CD-writer, this problem won't arise; just download directly onto CD-ROM.

You will need to take your own supply of CD-ROMs or floppies, as libraries and Internet cafés don't supply them. The advantage of a CD-ROM is the huge volume of graphics that it can hold – several hundred times the storage capacity of a floppy disk. Graphics can be stored permanently on a CD-ROM rather than on your hard drive, where they would take up valuable space and slow down the performance of your whole system.

I have been using computer-printed patterns and images for some time with absolutely no problem at all. With some printers you may have to use the special media setting. When I require a very clear image I print it using the photographic paper setting and set it at a high resolution. However, for most purposes this is unnecessary – in fact, when the colours are a little paler it gives the impression of age to the fabric.

If you have a flat-bed scanner any image is usable, but if you intend to sell any of your pieces, always check that you aren't infringing anyone's copyright. There are many sources of copyright-free material, many free images on the Internet, and museums and university departments sometimes have images of antique textiles and wallpapers which you can download. You will probably only be able to download a small segment of the pattern, in which case you will have to do some work using a drawing program to match and build the image. However, the fun and sense of achievement in getting the image to just the right size far outweighs the frustration of any mistakes. Just remember to save your work regularly.

A COMPUTER-PRINTED SCENE

EQUIPMENT AND MATERIALS
Computer and monitor
Colour inkjet printer (laser printers are not suitable for this method)
Flat-bed scanner (optional)
Fabric
Avery labels

AVERY LABELS

Avery labels are made from firm paper designed for use in a printer. The paper has a sticky surface, which is covered with a non-stick backing. Used for normal purposes, the backing is left on the label until after printing, but for our purposes, the backing is removed before printing, so that the fabric can be stuck to the label. The fabric thus becomes the front face of the label instead of the paper.

Avery A4 labels (code: L7167) are available from most good stationers and if they don't stock them, they will almost certainly be able to order some for you. As they come in packs of 40, they are a little expensive for one-offs, but are extremely convenient and easy to use. If you are part of a miniatures group, you may be able to share a packet to reduce the cost. If you don't want to use labels, you can mount your fabric on paper using a re-positionable spray adhesive, but in this case the paper can't be re-used. After one use, most of the stickiness will be lost; spraying on more adhesive will make the fabric lumpy and uneven and, as the glue will not penetrate the paper sufficiently to dry to the correct level of stickiness, risks glue getting onto the fabric.

AVERY LABEL, FABRIC SUITABLE FOR PRINTING AND STIFFENING FABRICS FOR BACKING

THE PROCESS OF PRINTING

Using Avery labels

1 Lay your fabric on a flat surface, right-side down; if your fabric has no obvious right side, either side will do.

2 Peel the backing from a label and set the backing safely aside: after printing, the fabric can be removed and the backing re-applied to the label for future use. Place the label on the fabric, sticky side down. Turn the fabric over and smooth it out.

3 Trim the fabric back to the size of the label, making sure there are no loose threads: loose threads can jam your printer. Set aside until needed.

4 Check again for any stray threads and cut off any that have appeared.

5 Check which way the printer feeds the paper – i.e. does it print on the side that is facing up or the side that is facing down – then remove all the paper that is in the printer and place your fabric-covered paper in the intake tray so that it will print on the fabric side.

6 Print off your design.

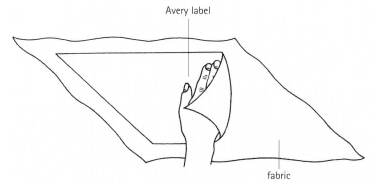

Avery label

fabric

SMOOTH DOWN AVERY LABELS AS YOU STICK THEM TO THE FABRIC

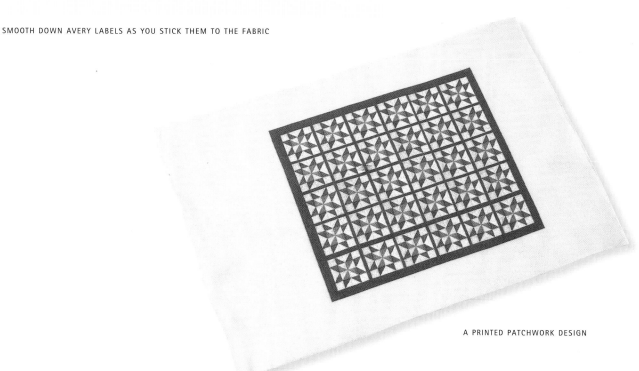

A PRINTED PATCHWORK DESIGN

EQUIPMENT
AND MATERIALS

Bin liner

Newspapers

Scissors

Copier paper

Repositionable spray adhesive

Fabric

Using repositionable spray adhesive

1 Split a large bin liner to form a sheet. Lay it on the floor or a large tabletop and cover it with several layers of newspaper.

2 Place a sheet of copier paper on the newspaper and spray it lightly with adhesive from a distance of 30cm (12in), keeping the spray can moving constantly. If the can is not moved, the glue will pool in one area, resulting in an uneven coating. Make sure you spray over the edges of the copier paper. Do not wet the paper with too much glue or it will soak into the fabric, giving it a rubbery texture when dry.

3 Immediately after spraying the paper, cover it with your fabric and place this fabric-covered paper on a clean, flat surface. Smooth the fabric down to ensure that it has adhered completely to the paper and also to remove any creases and wrinkles.

4 Check that all the edges of the fabric are stuck down, then trim the fabric back to the paper size. Make sure there are no loose threads anywhere. Place the trimmed fabric under a book to keep it flat until it is required.

5 To finish, follow steps 4–6 for using Avery labels.

Tips on 1/12 scale design

❦ In a full-size quilt, all the stitches would be very simple running stitches. In miniature, even a very tiny running stitch would be too big – the design definition would be lost. Therefore, I use a small, but not tiny, backstitch. This makes the quilting line continuous and helps define the design.

❦ Scaling down full-size designs for miniature quilting would make the stitching lines too close together to give the desired effect: it is the shadows created by the stitches that give a

quilting pattern life. Such close stitching would also cause the fabric to stiffen and flatten.

❦ Don't use a magnifying glass to work: this will have the same effect as above. Don't worry about scale; decide what size quilt you want and try to fit your chosen design elements within that area, in an open and well-spaced manner. You may well need to modify your original plan considerably. Simple and well-spaced designs can have a dramatic impact in miniature.

WEBSITES

There are several websites dedicated solely to miniatures. These are owned by very generous people who offer a wide range of free graphics. Two sites that I visit regularly are:

• Eileen's printables at http://www.members.home.net/eileen morgan/printables.html
• Jim's printable minis at http://www.printmini.com

I recommend both. They are well worth a visit in themselves and also provide links to other sites. 'Eileen's printables' has some very good rugs, exceptional quilts and beautiful wallpapers. Eileen has very kindly allowed me to include one of her rug designs in this book. You will find instructions for printing and finishing it under Eileen's green rug (see p 66).

'Jim's printable minis' contains images of everything from maps to microwave ovens, all of them excellent. His site includes patterns for rugs and quilts; he has also been generous enough to give his permission for me to include this pattern. To finish it, follow the instructions for the patchwork quilt on p 62.

Unless you have an Internet service that is not metered, I recommend downloading your chosen graphics: you can then print them off line.

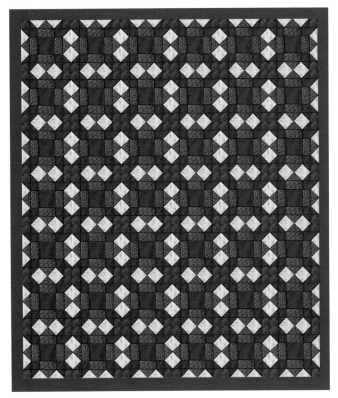

JIM'S QUILT PATTERN

PATCHWORK QUILT

I kept this sample very simple and quilted a line where the seams would be on a traditionally pieced quilt. This is known as 'in the ditch quilting'.

1 Set up your fabrics to work with or without a frame, as you choose.

2 Machine either side of the green 'joining' strips, using an invisible thread and a short machine stitch (stitch length No. 2). This leaves the finished quilt a little stiffer than hand sewing, but as it is very difficult to get even an unquilted miniature cover to drape realistically, the result is acceptable, and having the quilt a little stiffer will help it stay in

whatever position you wish to place it. If you do prefer a softer finish, hand stitch with a matching thread. Start all the hand stitching from the centre and work out to the edges using a small backstitch. Sew up to and around the inside of the outer green border, but do not sew around the outer edge.

3 Remove the quilt from the frame, if you are using one. Along one side, ease the front and back fabrics away from the wadding around the outer edge. Trim the wadding back as close as you can get to the last row of stitches. Repeat on the remaining three sides.

4 Cut the front and back fabrics to within 3mm (⅛in) of the outside green border on all four sides.

EQUIPMENT AND MATERIALS

Embroidery frame
Pins
Assa pins
Sewing needles
Sewing machine
Scissors
Paper
Embroidery frame (optional)
Cotton lawn
Backing fabric
Wadding
Embroidery cotton
Silver sand

THE FINISHED QUILT

MY DESIGN FOR A PATCHWORK QUILT

5 Fold the excess 3mm (⅛in) of white edge on your printed fabric to the inside, do the same on the backing fabric, then pin or tack the two folded edges.

6 Whip stitch the two fabrics together along one long and one short edge to form an 'L' shaped tube. Pin the tube closed at one end. (Whip stitching is simply oversewing the edges with small stitches.)

7 Make a cone shape with a small piece of paper. Place the narrow, open end of the cone into the open end of the 'L' shaped tube and fill it with dry silver sand. If the sand doesn't go around the corner, pin the edge that you have just filled closed, fill the rest of the tube from the other end, then pin that end closed.

8 Fold and stitch the remaining long edge, then fill as for the first.

9 Fold and stitch the remaining short edge and close completely. To help the top edge drape over the pillow, do not fill this with sand.

NB: Do not iron your quilt after finishing: this would flatten the texture you have so patiently created.

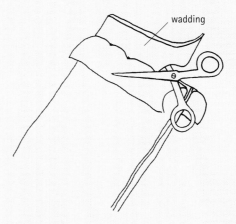

EASE THE FABRICS BACK FROM THE OUTER EDGE AND TRIM THE WADDING

PINNING THE TWO FOLDED EDGES TOGETHER

FILLING THE 'L' SHAPED TUBE WITH SAND

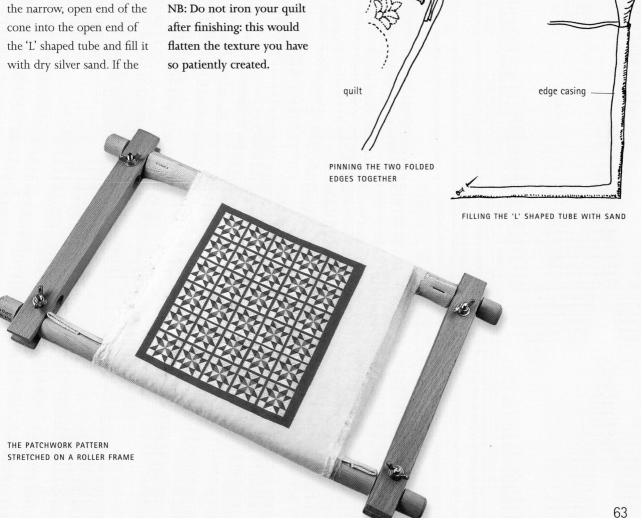

THE PATCHWORK PATTERN STRETCHED ON A ROLLER FRAME

DURHAM QUILT

Traditionally, a Durham quilt is made from a complete piece of cloth, rather than as a patchwork. Quilted covers can also be seen with broad stripes; these are known as stripy quilts.

In the past, the makers of Durham quilts often used a crayon for marking, and traces of crayon can be seen on some antique quilts. The people who made these quilts often needed the extra income gained from either selling a finished quilt or marking a pattern onto the fabric for someone else to sew. They were designed and marked with great skill and artistry by both men and women, although it was more frequently the women and girls of the household who did the sewing. Full-size versions of Durham quilts should be treated as national treasures and preserved carefully, not just for their beauty but because of the social history they represent.

A true Durham quilt can be of any colour, but the backing is often in a colour that contrasts with that on the front. In this example I used white for both sides – a style that would have been kept for special occasions.

A MINIATURE DURHAM QUILT

DESIGN FOR DURHAM QUILT

1 Scan the design for the Durham quilt and print it onto the cotton lawn in 12% black (pale grey). This printing should virtually disappear when it is stitched over but will add to the shadow effect. If your quilt is going to be made in any colour other than white, it is a good idea to print the pattern in a shade darker than that of your fabric. Alternatively, trace it with a water-soluble transfer pencil or pen and iron it onto your fabric.

2 Set the fabric for sewing with or without a frame (see pp 54 and 55). Sew with a small back-stitch, starting at the centre and working out towards the border. Once you have worked the scalloped border, release the quilt from the frame (if you have used one).

3 Cut the two fabrics to within 12mm (½in) of the scalloped border and cut the wadding to within 6mm (¼in) of the scallops.

4 Fold the front fabric over the wadding and pin in place, then fold the backing fabric to the inside, so it comes to just short of the edge. Pin through all the layers.

5 Backstitch all around, as close to the edge as you can get, then work another row of backstitch 6mm (¼in) inside these edge stitches.

6 Wash out any residue from the transfer pencil and allow to drip dry. Do not iron your quilt as this will flatten and crush all the quilting and crease the surface, and all the shadowing created by the stitches will be lost.

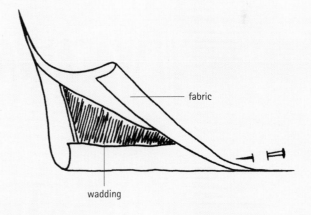

FOLD THE FABRICS OVER THE CUT
WADDING AND PIN IN PLACE

65

EQUIPMENT AND MATERIALS
Computer and monitor
Colour inkjet printer
Ruler
Iron
Flat-bed scanner (optional)
Scissors
Avery label or A4 inkjet paper and repositionable spray adhesive
Fabric with a pronounced weave
PVA adhesive
Vilene

EILEEN'S GREEN RUG

This rug design has been reproduced with the kind permission of Eileen Morgan. You can either scan the design and open the file in a draw or paint program, or log on to the Internet and download your chosen image. If you are using Microsoft Windows, save the file in a document folder as a bitmap image. To do this:

1 Click on 'file' on the toolbar

2 Click on the 'output wizard'; a dialogue box will open

3 Select 'Other file type'

4 Click on 'next'

5 Scroll down to 'Windows bitmap (*.btm)' and highlight

6 Click 'finish'

PATTERN FOR EILEEN'S GREEN RUG

Some drawing software won't recognize other image formats, but a bitmap is a safe bet with the majority of programs. Eileen's images are created in Microsoft's Paint program (which comes with Windows), so they are usually compatible. Once you have opened the image in your chosen program, you can modify it by intensifying the colours, altering the size, etc. Please don't forget to save your work regularly so you can backtrack if you make a mistake or change your mind.

THE FABRIC USED WILL AFFECT THE COLOURS OF THE FINISHED DESIGN

1 Prepare your fabric with either an Avery page label or repositionable spray adhesive (see p 59 or 60). Use a fabric with a pronounced weave; it doesn't need to be particularly thin.

2 Load your prepared fabric into your printer intake tray so that the image will be printed on the fabric side. To get a very sharp, highly saturated colour image, change the resolution to the highest dpi in your printer control program (be aware that this will use up a lot of ink). Alternatively, use the print setting for photograph-quality inkjet papers. The image will be paler, but you can darken the colours in your draw program.

3 Print the image.

4 When dry, remove the fabric from its backing and press with a hot, dry iron.

5 You should be able to just see the print through the fabric on the back of the rug.

6 Using a ruler, or other straight edge, run a line of PVA adhesive along the two short edges of the print, being careful not to get any glue on the unprinted areas of these two edges: glue here will make it virtually impossible to fray the edges to create a fringe.

7 Work the glue a little into the fibres.

8 Work more PVA into the fabric on the two long edges, this time covering the edge of the print and moving onto the unprinted fabric. Work the glue well into the fibres. Don't allow any glue to get onto the

front face of the print or it will spoil the appearance of the finished rug.

9 Allow the glue to dry thoroughly.

10 At the two short edges, cut the fabric to within 12mm (½in) of the printed area. This will form the fringe.

11 Fray the fabric by removing the threads that run parallel to the print. Fray right up to the edge of the print. At the two long edges, trim the fabric straight back to the edge of the print.

12 Cut a piece of Vilene to fit exactly between the two fringed edges but wider than the design, and press at the recommended temperature.

13 Trim the Vilene to fit exactly between the long edges of the rug.

14 Place on a flat surface to cool completely.

EILEEN'S RUG PATTERN, PRINTED

Needle punch
Embroidery hoop, 15–20cm (6–8in) in diameter
Embroidery needles
Scissors
Iron
Closely woven fabric, medium weight (polycotton is fine)
Embroidery cottons or silks, even sewing threads
Fabric tape
Vilene, medium weight

NEEDLE PUNCH RUG

This type of embroidery is also known as Russian punch. It is a very simple and effective means of creating a hooked rug. The secret is to make sure the thread always has free movement through the punch: the loops will not form properly if the thread is restricted in any way.

A needle punch is peculiar in the way that it is threaded. The needle is hollow and the thread goes straight up the centre from the pointed end. For this reason, needle punches are supplied with a long wire threader. Don't lose this: it is impossible to thread the punch without one. Punches come in a variety of sizes. Using the wrong size thread for the bore of your needle can make it difficult to use the needle punch; in fact, this is the most common reason for difficulties. If you want to use a thicker thread – and you can even use wool – use a thicker needle.

For this example I used a fine punch and worked the rug entirely in a single strand of embroidery cotton. I used colours left over from other projects; beige to outline the pattern, two colours for each diamond shape and a darker colour for the background. Choose yours to suit your décor.

1 Trace or print the outline pattern below onto your fabric. I traced the example to give me as much fabric as possible to fit into the hoop.

2 Centre the design over the inner ring of the hoop, place the outer ring over it and tighten the little screw on the edge. Tension the fabric as you do this, taking care to keep the lines of the pattern as straight as possible. The fabric must be drum-tight for this technique to be effective. It helps to wrap the inner ring with fabric tape before fitting the fabric as this gives added grip. If your punch is the adjustable type, set it at minimum.

USING TWO SHADES OF EACH
COLOUR FOR THE DIAMONDS
ADDS A SENSE OF DEPTH

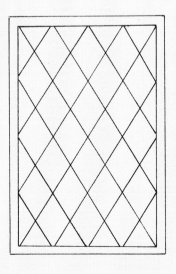

PATTERN FOR NEEDLE PUNCH RUG

3 Thread the needle punch as suggested in the enclosed instructions. If there are no instructions provided, thread the wire loop down from the top of the punch, exiting at the needle end. Put the thread through the loop at the end of the needle and pull it up through the centre of the punch, leaving a short tail of thread hanging out at the needle end.

4 Work the outline first. Push the needle through the fabric, withdraw it until the point only just clears the fabric, then re-insert one needle-width away from the previous puncture. Continue in this manner: work two rows of

punches along every line, leaving a needle-width gap between the rows. You will find that a loop forms on the underside of the fabric and a small stitch on the surface. When working the diamond shapes, work inwards towards the centre of each diamond. I worked four rounds of one colour, then changed to another colour to fill in the centre.

5 Cut the fabric, leaving a 6mm (¼in) allowance on all four sides. Fold these hems over and glue or sew them to the back of the rug.

6 Cut a piece of medium-weight Vilene to fit the back of your rug exactly and glue it in position. Iron the rug to help it lie flat and to sharpen the long edges.

Do not iron the surface directly, as you will flatten the pile you have created; there are special ironing sheets, available from haberdashers, that can be used for ironing velvet.

7 Whip stitch the edges, in your background colour, on all four sides. Set aside on a flat surface until the glue is completely dry.

ANOTHER DESIGN THAT WORKS WELL AS A NEEDLE PUNCH RUG

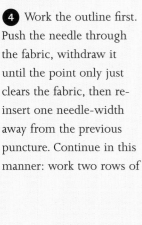

frame

rug design

excess fabric

THE MOUNTED RUG DESIGN

Decorative beading

There are a great many types and shapes of beads available for embroidery; unfortunately, very few of them are suitable for use in miniature textiles. Those most commonly used are the Japanese size 15, followed by Japanese size 12 and accent beads. The size 15 beads are sold by miniatures' stores for use in dolls' houses, but I consider them far too big for true 1/12 scale. Beads nearer the scale (size 24 I believe) used to be made in Czechoslovakia, but these are now impossible to find, unless someone has an old stock of them. This means we are stuck with the size 15, until some enterprising company reintroduces the size 24.

Accent beads provide an alternative but as they don't have a hole in them, you have to glue them in position. They come in a wide variety of colours, are very reasonably priced, and you get a lot for your money. Top of my wish list is for someone to put holes in them. I have found it effective to use accent beads and larger beads together in one design: this makes the larger beads seem more in scale, and their use intentional. Glue stiffens fabric a little, but spot design minimizes this effect. Spot design uses small amounts of beads or embroidery, or both, to provide an accent to a design, for example, a pearl attached to the centre of a flower or a line of beads used to highlight a bodice or neckline.

A SELECTION OF SIZE 15
JAPANESE BEADS

SEED AND ACCENT BEADS USED TO
HIGHLIGHT LACE EDGINGS

ACCENT BEADS COME
IN A HUGE RANGE OF COLOURS

STORING YOUR BEADS IN CLEAR CONTAINERS WILL
MAKE IDENTIFICATION MUCH QUICKER

ATTACHING SEED BEADS

Seed beads are round beads with a hole. They are widely available in a variety of sizes, from 6/00 to 15/00; the larger the number, the smaller the bead. Beads can be attached to fabrics using any of the following methods:

Sewing on individually

The beads are picked up and sewn onto the fabric one at a time.

Couching

The beads are strung onto a thread, laid around the design lines and attached with a small stitch taken over the thread between each bead.

Knitting in

The beads are strung onto the ball thread (i.e. the thread still attached to the ball of wool, skein of cotton, etc.) and after each stitch, one bead is drawn up before the next stitch is worked.

Crochet

This is worked in the same way as for knitting, with one bead drawn up after each crochet stitch.

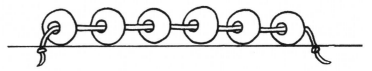

Step 1: anchor a loosely strung length of beads to the fabric with a knot at each end

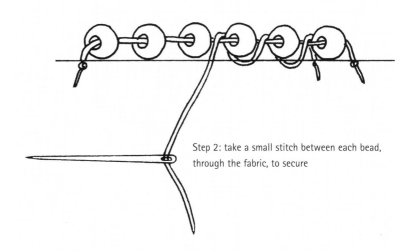

Step 2: take a small stitch between each bead, through the fabric, to secure

COUCHING BEADS

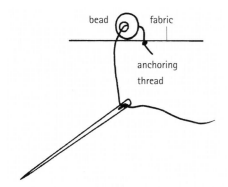

bead   fabric

anchoring thread

ATTACHING A SINGLE BEAD

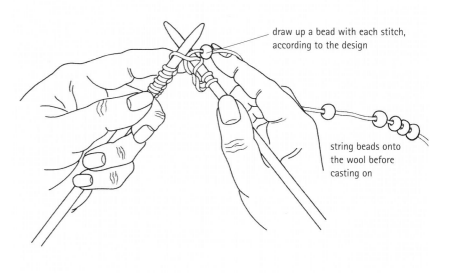

draw up a bead with each stitch, according to the design

string beads onto the wool before casting on

KNITTING IN BEADS

Weaving

Weaving is usually done on a small bead loom. The beads for each row are strung onto the weaving thread and the thread then passed under the warp threads to the opposite side of the loom. One bead is then positioned between each warp thread and the weaving thread passed back through each bead and over each warp thread. Bead weaving is a more specialized area of decoration and there are many very good books on the subject. It is most often used to make purses, belts and decorative panels.

Any cross stitch or needlepoint chart can be used for bead weaving; simply substitute one bead for each stitch in the appropriate colour. If your loom is very small, you will need to weave your pattern in sections, then sew them together.

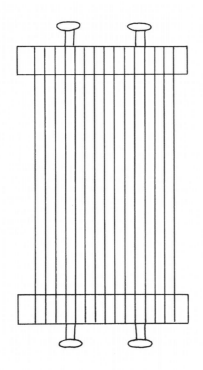

STEP 1: WARP THE BEAD LOOM, WITH ONE MORE WARP THREAD THAN THE NUMBER OF BEADS REQUIRED

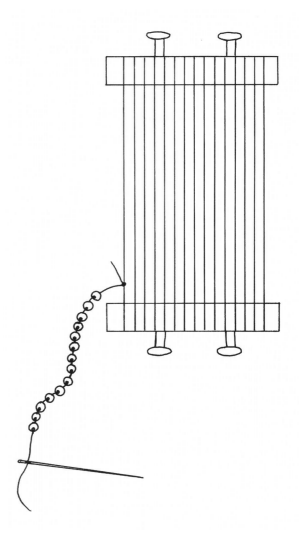

STEP 2: TIE YOUR THREAD TO THE FIRST WARP ROW ON THE LEFT, WITH ALL THE BEADS FOR THAT ROW THREADED IN SEQUENCE

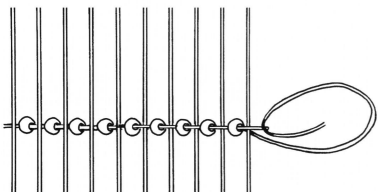

Tambour beading

This is my personal favourite. It is very simple and uses minimal equipment. Tambour embroidery is embroidery executed with a hook. The fabric is stretched taut in an embroidery hoop, hence the name – tambour means drum. It is particularly suitable for free-flowing forms of embroidery and for attaching beads. Quick to work, it forms a chain stitch on the surface and a small running stitch on the underside. (When beading, the underside is the right side.)

STEP 3: TAKE THE NEEDLE, THREAD AND BEADS UNDER ALL OF THE WARP THREADS THEN WIGGLE THE BEADS SO THAT ONE LIES BETWEEN EACH PAIR OF WARP THREADS

FOR TAMBOUR EMBROIDERY, THE FABRIC IS STRETCHED TIGHT IN AN EMBROIDERY FRAME. IF THE FABRIC IS FINE, USE A LAYER OF STABILIZING FABRIC TO ADD BODY

STEP 4: PASS THE NEEDLE BACK THROUGH THE HOLES OF THE BEADS, THIS TIME TAKING IT OVER THE WARP THREADS. WORK THE SECOND AND SUBSEQUENT ROWS IN THE SAME WAY

TAMBOUR EMBROIDERY

EQUIPMENT
AND MATERIALS

Tambour hook and handle
(available from
lace-making suppliers)
Embroidery hoops × 2,
1 large, 1 medium
Embroidery stand (tambour
embroidery is worked using
both hands, so a stand
is essential and must grip
the hoop firmly)
Cotton tape
Fabric
Embroidery thread

Tambour embroidery was a favourite of Victorian women. They considered the craft an excellent way of showing off their elegant hands to guests – particularly the male kind. During the Victorian period there were workshops devoted to this skill. These were staffed entirely by young girls who developed a high degree of artistry and speed in their work. They worked long hours for poor pay, but even so, it became too expensive to apply the level of decoration and embellishment expected by wealthy Victorian ladies and the art survived only as a parlour and drawing room craft for young ladies with plenty of free time.

Preparation

Choose a transparent fabric for practice – even nylon will do, providing it has no stretch. This will allow you to see what your hands and the hook are doing. Wrap the inner ring of your embroidery hoop with ordinary cotton tape. This will help to prevent the fabric from slipping and keep it taut while you work. The stitch is worked directly from the reel of thread.

THE SPECIAL HOOK USED FOR
TAMBOUR BEADING AND EMBROIDERY

Starting off: the traditional method

Note that the hook has been drawn larger than true scale, for clarity.

1 Pierce the fabric with hook facing left.

2 Lay the thread over the hook.

3 Turn the hook until it faces right.

4 Draw a thread loop through the fabric.

5 Turn the hook to the left, pierce the fabric and lay the cut end of the thread over the hook.

6 Turn the hook to the right and take the cut end through the fabric and also through the loop formed in the previous stitch.

7 Tighten the end into a knot.

8 Turn the hook left and pierce the fabric a little way from the knot.

9 Lay the bottom thread over the hook.

10 Turn the hook to the right and draw a loop to the surface. You are now ready to start stitching.

Starting off: an easy alternative

1 Thread a sewing needle with your chosen thread; do not cut it free of the reel.
2 Pierce the fabric from below and take a few tiny stitches to anchor the thread.
3 Follow steps 5–10 of the traditional method to begin your tambour embroidery.

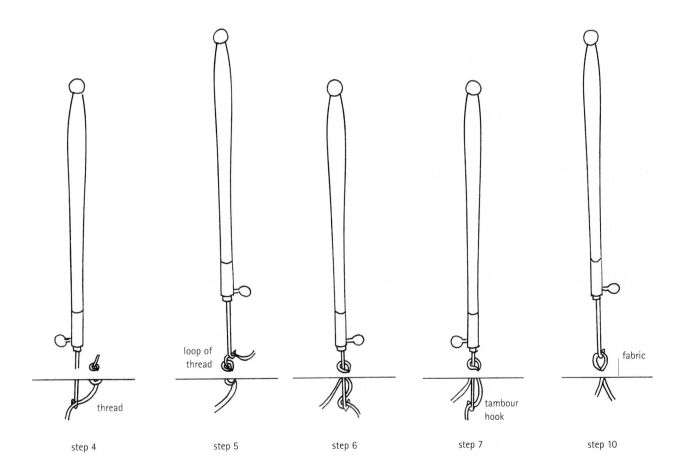

| step 4 | step 5 | step 6 | step 7 | step 10 |

thread · loop of thread · tambour hook · fabric

STARTING OFF A THREAD FOR TAMBOUR EMBROIDERY

Working the stitch

1 With the starting loop on the hook and the hook facing left, pierce the fabric. Lay the lower thread over the hook, rotate the hook to the right and draw a loop to the surface through the starting loop. To ease the hook up through the fabric and loop it, it may help to lean the handle a little to the left. Practice until you can work the tambour hook in any direction with ease.

2 Hold the new loop on the hook and rotate to the left.

3 Pierce the fabric a short distance from the last puncture. Lay the thread over the hook, rotate the hook to the right, draw up through the last loop formed, and rotate the hook to the left. You will now be starting to form a chain stitch on the surface.

4 Continue as for steps 1–3.

Fastening off: the traditional method

1 Make a slightly longer chain stitch, then turn the hook to the right.

2 Pick up the previous chain through the long loop and pull the underneath thread to tighten the knot.

3 Make a stitch in the same place, pick up the previous chain as before, then tighten the thread from below.

4 Bring a final chain to the surface and cut the loop.

5 Draw the reel thread out from the work.

Fastening off: an easy alternative

1 Leave the final loop on the hook, on the surface of your fabric.
2 Cut the working thread underneath, leaving a long strand, and thread this onto a sewing needle.
3 Bring the sewing needle to the surface, through the last loop worked.
4 Pull the loop tight and take a few small stitches to secure.

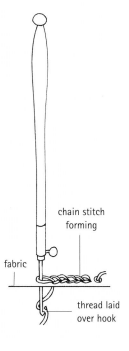

chain stitch forming

fabric

thread laid over hook

FORMING A CHAIN STITCH

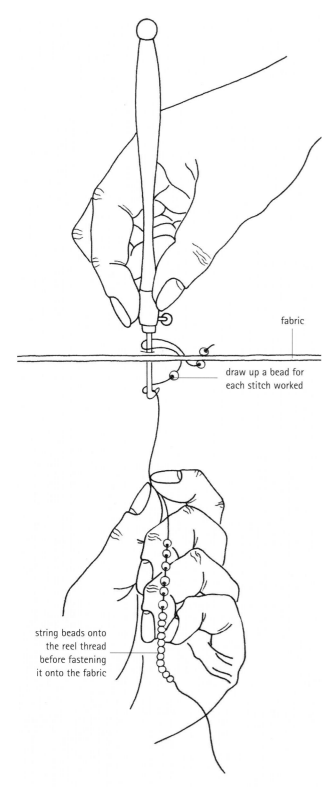

fabric

draw up a bead for
each stitch worked

string beads onto
the reel thread
before fastening
it onto the fabric

ATTACHING BEADS BY TAMBOUR EMBROIDERY

Attaching beads

This method of attaching beads is very simple and quick. The beads are attached on the underside of the embroidery hoop – a factor to be taken into consideration when mixing beads with embroidery. You will need to turn the hoop over to work the embroidery, so a little forward planning when transferring the design to the fabric will help with the smooth working of your pattern. The method is the same as for tambour embroidery, with the addition of two steps:

1 thread the beads onto the reel thread before you fasten it to the fabric; and

2 push a bead up to the work before you loop the thread over the hook.

A WEDDING GOWN

EQUIPMENT AND MATERIALS

Fabric stabilizer (water-soluble) or vanishing muslin
Embroidery hoops × 2, 1 2.5cm (1in) the other not less than 20cm (8in)
Embroidery hoop holder, floor-standing if possible
Tambour hook
Sewing needle
Beading needle
Scissors
Clingfilm
Pins
Screwdriver or pliers
Book or stiff card
Soft pencil
Soft toothbrush
Doll
Silk chiffon, ivory, 50cm (20in)
Medium-weight silk, white, 50cm (20in)
Stabilizing fabric, 50cm (20in)
Pearl beads, the smallest you can find
Madeira thread No. 70, white (this is fine, but very strong)
Cotton lace
Silk ribbon
Sewing thread
Polyester wadding
PVA adhesive

The doll

With the doll I bought, it was possible to choose from a range of different arms and legs. For this design I have chosen full arms and half legs. This gave me the option of making a very slim doll.

1 Make your doll according to the supplied instructions. Cover the join between the porcelain and fabric with a small piece of cotton lace, slotted with 2mm (¹⁄₁₆in) silk ribbon, and slip stitch it into place. This will avoid the added bulk of drawers, and the added task of making them.

2 Stuff the legs with wadding so that they are firm but fill the body more lightly. Wrap a thread around the waist and pull tight to give the doll a smaller and more defined waist line. Trim off the excess fabric and glue the legs into the body cavity. It is important to let the glue dry completely – do not be tempted to disturb it as this will weaken the bond.

3 Make the doll up to a finished height of 14cm (5½in). If your doll is already wigged, wrap some clingfilm loosely around her hair to keep it tidy; if not, apply the wig once your doll is fully dressed.

WEDDING GOWN AND VEIL WITH BEADWORK DESIGNS

The skirts

This pattern is very simple, but you will need to adjust the bodice after fitting it to the doll in order to compensate for differences in the slimness of the doll when it is made up. Any patterns for 1/12 scale dolls' clothes can be adapted for tambour work.

1 For this dress, the first step is to make up the petticoat and fit it to the doll. You need a lot of fabric for such a tiny dress in order to fit the hoops. Hem around the bottom, sew up the back seam, then turn right-sides out. Sew a gathering thread around the waist edge, fit the petticoat to the doll, draw up the gathers and fasten off the thread to anchor the stitches.

2 Cut one piece of silk chiffon and one piece of stabilizing fabric, both 35cm (14in) square.

3 Lay the chiffon on a flat surface and cover it with the stabilizing fabric, being careful to match edge to edge. Pin or tack these pieces together.

4 Lay these fabrics over the inner ring of the largest embroidery hoop, chiffon side down.

5 Fit the outer ring over this and tighten the screw until it just grips. Remove the pins or tacks and, working around the outside, begin to gently pull the chiffon and stabilizer, separately, in order to tighten them. Gradually tighten the screw on the hoop as you do this until it won't go any further. Use a screwdriver or pliers to finish. Both fabrics should be drum-tight.

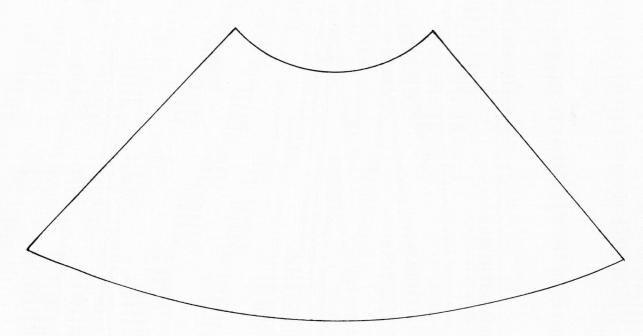

PATTERN FOR PETTICOAT

French seams

With wrong sides together, sew up the seam close to the edge. Trim close to the stitching and press the seam. Turn the wrong side out and seam again, making sure the raw edges are within the stitched seam.

6 Trace off the designs for the hem decoration and the skirt embroidery. Trim this tracing to fit inside the recess on the underside of the hoop. Make sure that each end of the tracing is close to the sides of the embroidery hoop; this will result in the pattern area being well below the centre of the hoop. Pin in place.

7 Place something firm, for example a book or a stiff piece of card, below the tracing and trace the pattern onto the top surface of the stabilizing fabric. The markings will disappear when the stabilizer dissolves. Use a soft pencil – do not use an ink pen or you risk marking the chiffon and dissolving the stabilizer before you have worked the pattern.

8 Remove the tracing and mount the hoop on an embroidery stand or support.

ALTERNATIVE EMBROIDERY DESIGN FOR SKIRT

EMBROIDERY DESIGN FOR SKIRT

DESIGN FOR HEM DECORATION

9 Work three rows of tambour beading at the hem edge. Turn the hoop over and, from the correct side, work the tambour embroidery with the white Madeira thread. The pattern should show through the fabric enough to work the embroidery. If you have any problems seeing the pattern, position your sewing light at a low angle so that it shines up through the fabric or deepen the pencil lines on the reverse.

10 When your beading is complete, remove the fabrics from the hoop and rinse them thoroughly in water, making sure that all the stabilizer has been removed. You will know when it has gone – all the pencil marks will disappear. It helps to use a soft toothbrush gently around the beads.

11 Allow the fabrics to dry naturally or, to save time, dry them with a hair dryer, then press carefully.

12 Finish the overskirt by straightening the side and top edges. At the beaded edge, cut the fabric to within 6mm (¼in) of the lowest row of beads, following the curves of the

pattern. Carefully snip into each curve, fold up the excess fabric and slip stitch in place.

13 Seam the two short edges of the overskirt. It is best to use French seaming for this as it gives a sealed seam, with all the raw edges enclosed.

14 Cut a piece of white silk to the same width as the chiffon overskirt but 12mm (½in) longer. Following the same curvature as for the overskirt, turn a 6mm (¼in) hem, and seam the two short edges, again, as for the overskirt.

15 Put the underskirt inside the overskirt, matching the seams and top edge. Sew the top edges together with a row of small running stitches, leaving a fairly long thread.

16 Fit the skirts to your doll, draw up the gathers evenly (working in more gathers on the back), wind the excess thread around the waist of the doll, pull it tight and fasten off.

17 Add a few decorative touches to the overskirt before fitting the skirts to the doll. (On this example

Ladder stitch

Take a small anchoring stitch then, parallel to it and a short distance away, take another small stitch. Without drawing these tight, take a third small stitch beneath the first, anchoring stitch. Work several stitches following this pattern. Hold the fabric firmly draw up all the loose thread. This will draw the parallel stitches together and should form an invisible seam on the surface of the fabric.

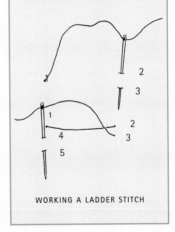

WORKING A LADDER STITCH

I have added little bows to the top row of beading and embroidered little daisies, with a bead in the centre, all over the overskirt.)

Bodice and sleeves

1 Set up the hoop again, this time with white silk.

2 Trace the pattern pieces for the front bodice, back

bodice (only one side is shown; reverse the pattern for the second side) and both sleeves (reverse the pattern for the second sleeve) onto the fabric. There is no need to use stabilizer as the fabric is firm enough not to distort when working the embroidery. The broken lines on the bodice, sleeves and back show the position of the beading.

3 If you wish, add a little tambour embroidery to the bodice front as far up as the top of the darts; any higher and it will interfere with making up the dress. When you have finished, release it from the hoop.

4 Cut out the pattern pieces, leaving a 6mm (¼in) seam allowance.

5 Cut a second back piece, the reverse of the beaded piece. Sew up the darts, then fold over and sew the excess fabric at the beaded edges.

6 Repeat step 5 with the beaded edges of the sleeve and back.

7 Sew the back and fronts together at the sides and shoulders.

8 Turn up and slip stitch the bottom edges of the sleeves.

9 Sew up the sleeve seams from the top edge to the elbow (just above the beads).

10 Sew a line of gathers at the top, arched part of the sleeves.

11 Set the sleeves into the bodice. For each, with the sleeve right-side out and the bodice wrong-side out, centre the gathered part of the sleeve on the shoulder seam of the bodice with the right sides together. Backstitch all around the armhole on the wrong side of the bodice. Trim the excess fabric back to the seam line and turn the bodice right-side out.

12 Fit the bodice to the doll, with the beaded edge of the back overlapping the unbeaded edge. Close the bodice with slip stitch and pull tight. Take up any loose areas with ladder stitching.

13 On the lower back edge of the bodice, using a needle or a pair of closed, pointed scissors, fold the raw edge under.

14 Finally, attach the bodice to the skirt waist with slip stitch.

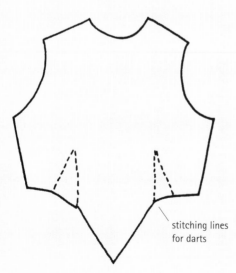

PATTERN FOR BODICE FRONT

stitching lines for darts

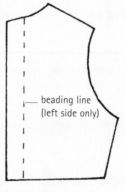

beading line (left side only)

PATTERN FOR BODICE BACK

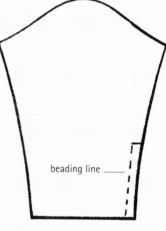

beading line

PATTERN FOR SLEEVES

Finishing off the dress

1 Cut a small piece of chiffon to fit the top of the bodice front and back. The chiffon should only reach halfway down the back and to the top of the darts on the front, but it must reach right up to the neck edge.

2 Cut two pieces of lace and gather each one by slotting a silk ribbon through it. Take one piece and draw up the ribbons until it fits the chiffon, from the beaded edge at the back, over the shoulder, to the centre of the front. It should follow and cover the edge of the chiffon. Slip stitch in place.

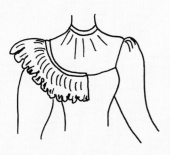

FITTING THE LACE RUFFLE OVER THE SHOULDER

3 Repeat with the second bit of lace for the other shoulder. Join the excess ribbon from each in a bow at the centre front.

4 Cut a piece of lace to fit around the neck edge of the bodice and slip stitch the edge of the lace to the edge of the neck, closing the lace up at the back of the neck.

5 Cut some silk ribbon to fit over the lace, slip stitch it to the edge of the neck and close it at the back.

The veil

1 Set up the largest hoop with silk chiffon and stabilizing fabric as before (see The skirts, p 81).

2 Trace the veil border onto the stabilizing fabric at the lowest point on the fabric that it will fit. Work a single row of beads along this.

3 Release the fabrics from the frame and finish

off the beaded edge in the same way as the chiffon overskirt. Next, trim each side edge straight and oversew the edges. The side edges should be long enough to reach from the top of the head to form a short train at the bottom.

4 Set up your embroidery hoop with a second length of chiffon and stabilizing fabric.

5 Using the same tracing as before, make a second veil, about one-third the length of the first. Before releasing this veil from the hoop, you need to make the headdress to attach the veil to.

6 To make the headdress, transfer the oval shape given to an unused area of the chiffon and cover the three ovals with tambour beading.

7 Now remove the fabrics from the hoop, and rinse thoroughly.

8 Once the stabilizer has been removed, fold under the excess fabric and slip stitch to secure.

9 Place the short veil over the long one, aligning their top edges. Gather both pieces of fabric as one and fasten to the headdress so that it comes two-thirds of the way up each side.

10 Either glue or sew the headdress and veil to the doll's hair and arrange in a pleasing drape.

BEADING DESIGN FOR HEADDRESS

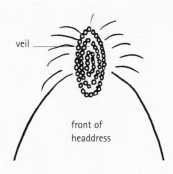

POSITION OF VEIL ATTACHMENT

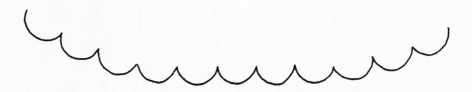

PATTERN FOR VEIL BORDER

ELIZABETHAN GOWN

EQUIPMENT AND MATERIALS

Sewing needles

Sewing threads

Small, pointed scissors

Scissors

Velvets, any colour except blue, which was reserved for the servant class

Silk brocade

Medium-weight plain silk

Fine cotton lawn (if making farthingale)

Gold tissue fabric

Covered wire

Assorted lace, braids (gold), silk ribbons and beads

Fine net

Ribbon, 12mm (½in) wide

Polyester wadding

Iron-on interfacing, medium weight

Iron-on interfacing, stiff*

Silk ribbon (for bum roll)

Bond-a-web

◎◎

* If you can't find a very stiff iron-on interfacing, use a non-iron one with Bond-a-web

This gown is typical of those worn by wealthy women of the mid-1580s, during the reign of Elizabeth I. The clothing of this period was very restrictive both for sitting and walking. Together with the corset, the bodice of the gown – stiffened with whalebone, steel or wood – made bending your back impossible. Sitting was impossible as well because of the width of the farthingale. It was the usual practice for ladies to use a stool, although they spent very little time actually sitting. In Elizabethan times, the concept of a comfortable chair was virtually unknown.

One sixteenth-century writer actually states that when young ladies began to wear their corsets for the first time, they pulled them in so tightly that 'they compressed their breasts so much that soon their breath began to stink'. I believe they were so tightly laced they were unable to draw a normal breath and so suffered from lung infections. Unfortunately, the doll I chose, with her porcelain half body and rather large bosom, is not as slender as she should be for this style of garment.

This style of dress is perfect for adorning with braids, beads and embroidery. The Elizabethans didn't know where to stop with their embellishment, so if you make this gown, go to town on it and enjoy yourself. If you don't want to make a farthingale, I have also included a pattern for a bum roll (yes, this is its real name). Bum rolls were worn instead of or as well as a farthingale.

Press all hems, seams, pleats and turnings as you make them: this will help to give a neater final appearance. All seams, unless otherwise stated, should be 3mm (⅛in).

THE DECORATION ON THE CLOTHING OF WEALTHY ELIZABETHANS WAS EXTRAVAGANT

The doll

If you have bought a kit doll, make it up following the instructions supplied. Ladies of the Elizabethan period normally shaved the front of their hair to give the appearance of a high forehead and wore wigs of bright colours. I have styled my doll's hair with tight curls at the front. The back, obscured by the hat, has a braid wound into a bun. This was a common Elizabethan style and is often seen in portraits of the period.

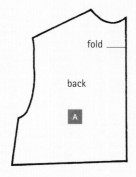

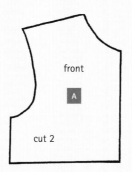

PATTERNS FOR CHEMISE FRONT AND BACK (CUT ON FOLDED FABRIC)

The chemise

While the chemise itself is not visible, it is necessary as the collar is attached to it.

1 Cut out both parts A in cotton lawn and sew up the side seams.

2 Fold under 3mm (⅛in) at the bottom edge and hem.

3 Sew the shoulder seams.

4 Turn under 3mm (⅛in) at the neck and armhole edges and fit to the doll.

5 Slip stitch the front edges together.

6 If you wish, sew a line of gathering stitches around the bottom edge, pull tight and fasten off.

Farthingale

1 Cut out pattern B in cotton lawn.

2 Cut a piece of very stiff interfacing to fit inside the waist area indicated.

3 If your wire isn't rigid enough not to become deformed while you handle it, twist two pieces together. Bend the wire to follow the curvature on the pattern and sew in place.

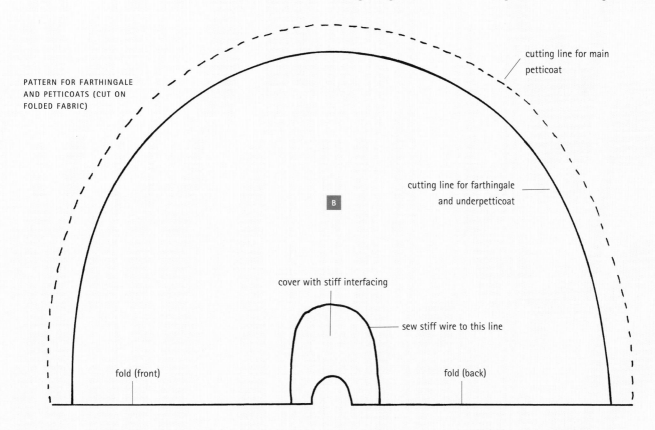

PATTERN FOR FARTHINGALE AND PETTICOATS (CUT ON FOLDED FABRIC)

cutting line for main petticoat

cutting line for farthingale and underpetticoat

cover with stiff interfacing

sew stiff wire to this line

fold (front)

fold (back)

4 Turn a 6mm (¼in) hem at the bottom edge.

5 Sew a row of gathering stitches around the waist edge, fit the farthingale to the doll, draw up the gathers and fasten off. The wire should be close to the waist of the doll at the front and standing out 12mm (½in) at the back; if not, pull the wire into shape.

Underpetticoat

1 Cut out pattern B in medium-weight silk.

2 Turn up a hem along the waist and bottom edges.

3 Sew a line of gathering stitches at the waist, fit the petticoat to the doll, draw up the gathers and fasten off. Make sure that most of the gathers are at the sides and back so the front of the skirts is as flat as possible.

Bum roll

1 Cut two pieces of fabric to the shape given in part C, adding a 3mm (⅛in) seam allowance.

2 With the right sides facing, sew the two pieces together with backstitch, leaving a small opening.

3 Turn right sides out, stuff lightly with wadding, then close the opening.

4 Sew two pieces of 2mm (¹⁄₁₆in) silk ribbon at the front edge, with which to tie the bum roll to the doll.

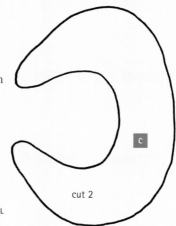

cut 2

PATTERN FOR BUM ROLL

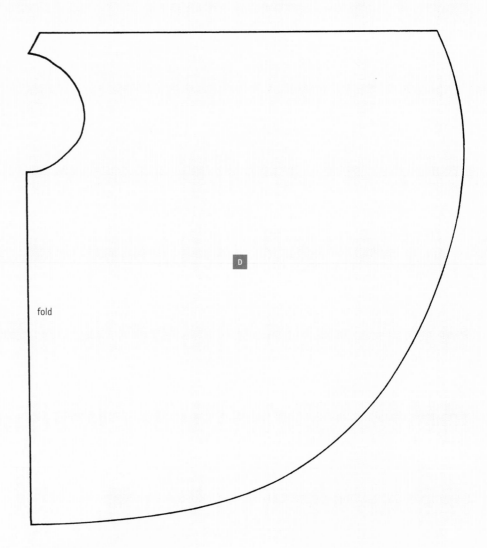

fold

PATTERN FOR OUTER SKIRT (CUT ON FOLDED FABRIC)

Main petticoat

1 For the main petticoat, cut out pattern B in silk brocade.

2 Turn up a hem at the waist and bottom edges.

3 Sew a line of gathering stitches at the waist edge, as for the under petticoat.

4 Fit to the doll and draw up the gathers. Arrange the gathers to the sides and back, trying to keep the front as flat as possible.

The outer skirt

1 Cut out pattern D in the velvet.

2 Turn up a 6mm (¼in) hem at the centre front.

3 Pleat the waist edge to fit the waist of the doll. Pin or tack down the length of the pleats, and steam press firmly on the wrong side.

4 Slip stitch the waist edge to the petticoats.

5 Slip stitch the front edges invisibly to the main petticoats. Arrange the pleats in a pleasing manner, then take one small invisible stitch halfway up each pleat to hold it in position.

6 Decorate the skirt with braid or trims of your choice. For this example, I cut the gold edging from a cheap lace and sewed it in place.

The inner sleeves

It was the practice not to sew in sleeves. Instead, both inner and outer sleeves had cord laces. The sleeves were attached to the bodice with these, and the lacings then covered with shoulder rolls.

1 Cut out four pieces of pattern E in the same fabric as the main petticoat. Do not cut into the darts or they will fray.

2 Sew up the outer seams of both sleeves.

3 Sew up all the darts; there are four on each sleeve.

4 Turn up 3mm (⅛in) at the wrist edges.

5 Sew the inner seams on both sleeves.

6 Sew a line of gathering stitches as indicated by the broken line on the pattern pieces.

7 Fit the sleeves to the doll and pad them out with a little wadding; the sleeves on a full-length gown are usually wired and padded, but in this instance padding is enough.

8 Draw up the gathers and slip stitch the sleeves to the armholes of the chemise.

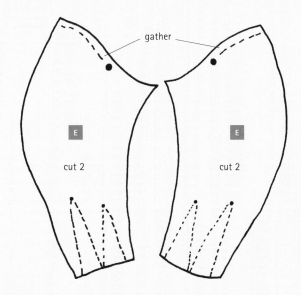

PATTERNS FOR INNER SLEEVES

In the name of fashion

This quotation from 1588 sums up the length people went to.

'... to become slender in wast [waist], and to have a straight spagnolised [Spanish in character] body, what pinching, what girding, what cingling [belting], will they not endure; yea sometimes with yron [iron] plates, with whalebones and other such trash, that their very skin, and quicke [living] flesh is eaten and consumed to the bones; whereby they sometimes worke their own death.

All high and more than human sciences are decked and enrobed with poeticall stile. Even as women make trunk sleeves of wyre, and whalebone bodices, backs of lathes [wood], stiff and bombasted verdugals, and to the open view of all men, paint and embellish themselves with conterfeit and borrowed beauties, so doth learning.'

Montaigne (essays translated by John Florio 1603) quoted in *Corsets and Crinolines*, Norah Waugh, Theatre Arts Books, 1990.

**PATTERN FOR
BODICE FRONT**

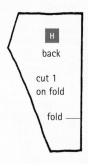

**PATTERN FOR
BODICE BACK**

**PATTERN FOR
BODICE SIDE**

The bodice

1 Cut out parts F, G and H in the fabric that you used for the outer skirts.

2 Iron stiff interfacing to both parts F and H, and medium-weight interfacing to part G.

3 Sew up the side seams between parts F and G and parts G and H, aligning the black dots on the patterns.

4 I used wonderful iron-on diamanté beads for decoration; if you wish to use these, apply them now.

5 Sew two lengths of very stiff wire to either side of the bodice front, 3mm (⅛in) in from the edge. Again, if your wire isn't stiff enough, twist two or more strands together.

6 Sew the shoulder straps to the back bodice at the position marked by the black dot.

7 Fit the bodice to the doll, and slip stitch the front opening closed.

8 Cover the stitches at the centre front opening with braid.

9 Apply braid to the waist edge of the bodice, around the back and down to the points at the front.

10 Pin the 12mm (½in) ribbon to the hem of the gown and begin to wind it smoothly around the skirt. Make sure the pleats are all in position and that the main petticoat is not creased. Continue winding the ribbon until you reach waist level, then pin the other end of the ribbon to the waist. Do not wrap it so

tightly that you crush the farthingale. Leave this ribbon on until the gown is finished. Wrapping the skirts in this way will help them to lie correctly.

The outer sleeves

1 Iron Bond-a-web to a piece of velvet large enough for both sleeves and remove the backing. (Because I used a gold-tissue fabric, I used the paper backing from the Bond-a-web to cover it

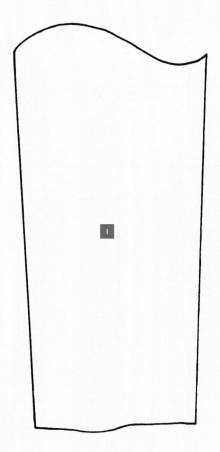

PATTERN FOR LEFT OUTER SLEEVE

before ironing, to prevent the iron from sticking to the tissue.)

2 Cut out the sleeves using pattern pieces I, and seal the fabric right up to the edges so that it doesn't fray. Use either a very dilute, watery PVA glue or Fray Check for this.

3 Sew the sleeve tops to the bodice, from the centre front of the bodice, right around the armhole, to meet again at the front.

cut 2

J

PATTERN FOR SHOULDER ROLL

The shoulder rolls

In Elizabethan gowns, shoulder rolls were usually padded but in a garment of this size, padding isn't necessary.

1 Cut out two pattern pieces J in velvet.

2 Fold the two long edges towards the centre, fold in half lengthways, and slip stitch closed. Repeat with the second piece.

3 Decorate the rolls with braids and ribbon bows.

4 Sew the rolls around the outer sleeves of the doll, angling them outwards at the top of the shoulder.

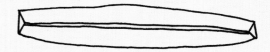

Step 1: fold one long edge over to the centre point

Step 2: fold the second long edge over in the same way

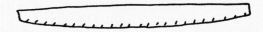

Step 3: fold the whole roll in half again, lengthways, and slip stitch the edges together

Step 4: roll the fabric between your thumb and index finger to move the seam to the centre of the roll

I

PATTERN FOR RIGHT OUTER SLEEVE

FOLDING THE SHOULDER ROLLS

The hat

Do not make the hat until your doll is wigged or it will not fit properly. I can't give an exact pattern for this hat due to variations in the sizes of dolls' heads and hairstyles.

1 Cut out parts K1 and K2 in velvet.

2 Turn down the back of the hat and sew the smaller piece to the larger, aligning a with a, b with b, and c with c, right sides together.

3 Turn the hat right-side out and try it for fit.

4 If necessary, trim around the front curves from a to c to reduce its size.

5 Sew a wire around the curved edges from a to c.

6 Turn over 3mm (⅛in) of fabric to cover the wire and slip stitch to secure.

7 Edge the hat with narrow silk ribbon.

8 Bend the wired edges to the correct shape and either glue, sew or pin the hat in place.

The standing collar

1 Using a small piece of net, cut out pattern piece L1, then cut out pattern piece L2 along the solid inner line.

2 Cut out motifs from a 6mm (¼in) piece of cotton lace and glue them around the edge of the net to the level of the broken outer line.

3 Cut out and glue a second row of motifs inside the first to create an all-over pattern.

4 Spray starch over both the collar and the support, and iron them to stiffen.

5 Sew the top curved edge of the support to the inner edge of the collar, right side of support to wrong side of collar.

6 Sew the bottom edge of the support to the neck edge of the chemise, right sides together.

7 Slip stitch the front of the standing collar closed.

Finishing off

1 Sew a short piece of lace around the wrist edge of the inner sleeves to represent cuffs.

2 Pull the outer sleeves to hang down the back of the gown, using a small, invisible stitch to hold them in place.

3 I made the forehead jewellery from wire and found items. Twist a short length of wire into a loop, glue a stone from a cheap bracelet to the centre, then thread a few pearls onto the wire, either side of the stone. Bend the wire to fit, and push it into your doll's hair.

4 The strung pearl necklaces are self-explanatory. You will need a minimum of three strands; Elizabethans often wore as many as six.

5 Add other decoration to your taste, including necklaces, bracelets, rings and bows...

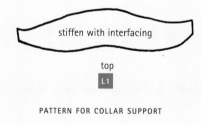

stiffen with interfacing

top
L1

PATTERN FOR COLLAR SUPPORT

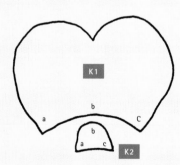

PATTERNS FOR HAT

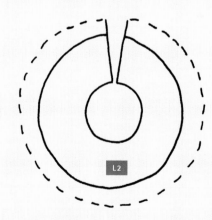

L2

PATTERN FOR STANDING COLLAR

SHAWL

Shawls such as this Victorian-style example were commonly worn over a white blouse. They had a hook-and-eye fastening, but this one is stitched closed. Shawls for evening wear were often lined with gold- or silver-tissue fabric.

I made this shawl using tambour beading and fringing, and added accent beads. I couldn't find any black silk chiffon so I used cream and painted it with silk paints. This type of shawl was also known as a shrug.

A BEADED SHAWL, VICTORIAN STYLE

1 Stretch your silk chiffon in an embroidery hoop (follow the instructions for Preparation under Tambour Embroidery, p 76).

2 Dilute 5ml (1tsp) of the silk paint with 100ml (3½fl oz) water – the paint should be very watery – to prevent it blocking the chiffon and losing its transparency.

3 Working over a sink or washing-up bowl, flood the paint onto the fabric with quick, sweeping strokes. If the brush is allowed to rest on the fabric, even briefly, the result will be patchy.

4 Prop the hoop on its edge to allow the excess liquid to drain as the fabric dries. There is no need to rinse.

5 If the fabric isn't dark enough, repeat this painting process until it is.

6 Once the painting is finished and the fabric is dry, remove it from the hoop and iron it with the iron set to silk. There is no need to hem at this stage, as the fabric will be returned to the hoop for beading.

7 Trace the beading design onto a piece of stabilizing fabric, then set up the hoop with the stabilizing fabric under the dyed chiffon.

8 Either attach the beads by sewing them to the chiffon face individually, or using a tambour hook to fix them to the stabilizing face (see p 77). Bead all the lines of the design.

PATTERN AND EMBROIDERY DESIGN FOR SHAWL

93

9 Remove the fabrics from the hoop and cut out the shape of the shawl, leaving a 3mm (⅛in) allowance all around.

10 Dissolve the stabilizing fabric by rinsing thoroughly in water.

11 To finish the edges, turn under the allowance and slip stitch in place.

Alternative edge finish

Roll the fabric edges between the thumb and index finger of your left hand and anchor the roll with small stitches. This is the traditional method of hemming chiffon and will give a neat finish.

Second alternative edge finish

1 Cut a piece of fine silk in a contrasting colour, following the shawl pattern and adding a 3mm (⅛in) allowance all around.

2 Sew both pieces together, right sides facing, leaving a small opening so that the shawl can be turned right-side out.

3 Turn right-side out, then close the opening with a few small stitches.

4 If you wish, oversew all the edges with a matching thread: at this stage, the shawl is very difficult to iron, and this will help to flatten the edges.

5 Work a fringe, using the smallest bugle beads you can find (see p 97).

6 Sew the fringe to the bottom edge of the shawl.

7 Arrange the shawl on your doll and slip stitch the front opening closed.

THE BRIDAL CAP

It was easy to shape this cap – I used a doll's head for modelling – but the beads gave me some problems. Suppliers gave me blank looks, long silences and a great deal of pity when I asked for tiny teardrop pearls. Needless to say, I was unable to find them. So I made them myself using a length of fine thread and oyster acrylic paint. I used the same thread to string the beads.

EQUIPMENT AND MATERIALS
Beading or sewing needle
Pin or cocktail stick
Fine tweezers
Scissors
Buckram, 102mm (4in) square
Silk, 102mm (4in) square
White lace
Fine thread
Accent beads, silver
Tiny beads, pearl or white
Acrylic paint, oyster
PVA adhesive

STRINGS OF BEADS DECORATE THE SIDES AND FRONT OF THE CAP

BASIC SHAPES OF BRIDAL CAP AND BACK PEAK

cap

back peak

FIX ACCENT BEADS TO THE TOP OF THE CAP, FOLLOWING THE PATTERN OF THE LACE

95

1 Cut a 203mm (8in) length of fine thread, making sure you have a clean, blunt cut at both ends – use sharp scissors.

2 Dip one end of the thread into the paint – a little droplet will form. It helps to twirl the thread a little while it is in the paint. It takes about five dips to build up a nice little teardrop shape. Allow the paint to dry between successive dips.

3 Dip both ends of the thread in this way, then cut it in half.

4 Repeat steps 2 and 3 until you have the required number of lengths. Set these aside.

5 Wet the buckram until it is soaking, floppy and soft; using warm water will help to speed up this process. Stretch and mould it over your doll's head, tie it in place, and leave to dry thoroughly.

6 While the cap is still on the doll, stretch the silk over it and glue around the edges to hold it in place.

7 With a light pencil line, mark the hairline on the buckram, then remove

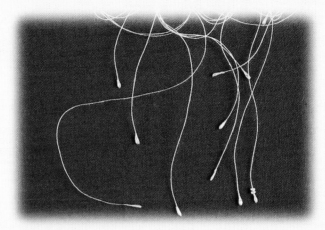

MY HOME-MADE TEARDROP BEADS

it from the doll to trim it to the pencil line. Tidy up the raw edges, then cover the cap with lace.

8 To make the back peak, cut a small semicircle of buckram, wide enough to reach around to the back of the doll's neck to within 3mm (⅛in) of each ear, and with a 6mm (¼in) radius.

9 Cover the back peak with silk and lace and sew it into position.

10 Returning to your home-made teardrop beads, thread each length, one at a time, onto the needle, keeping the teardrop at the bottom. Thread the remaining beads for each string onto this. All the front strings are the same length and all the neck nape strings are the same length. The long

loops on each side should match each other. Sew each string onto the cap as it is made, spacing them by the width of the largest bead.

11 Attach each bead string to the cap with a couple of small stitches.

12 Using a large pin or cocktail stick, apply small dots of PVA to the cap, following the pattern of the lace, and sprinkle with accent beads. Gently tap the beads with your clean fingertip to fix them to the glue, then shake the cap to remove any excess beads. Work just one small area at a time so that the glue doesn't dry before you apply the beads. Move the beads around before the glue dries to improve the design. Use a pair of fine tweezers to remove any beads that are not in the correct position.

96

BEADED LAMPSHADE FRINGE

For this project I used a bought table lamp. Beading works very well with this style of lamp. The finished piece would fit very nicely in a Victorian or Edwardian setting.

The shade had a scalloped edge but I filed this off: although it is possible to add a fringe to scallops, it is easier to attach one to a level edge. To work the fringe I used a small bead loom to support the attachment tape. If you don't have one, you can work the fringe without, it is just more difficult to handle.

1 Cut a length of bunka to measure the lampshade. Wrap it around the outside of the shade, and cut it to fit exactly.

2 Tie and stretch a second, longer piece of bunka across the loom or frame. I found it easier to work from left to right, but the choice is yours.

3 Attach your working thread to the bunka with a small knot and a stitch.

4 For each bead tassel, thread the beads onto your working thread in the following order:

1 size 15 gold
1 small bugle
1 size 15 gold
1 size 15 dark blue
1 size 11 antique gold
1 size 15 dark blue

Pass the needle straight through the centre of each

bead except the last (in this project, a dark blue size 15). Turn this bead so that the holes are at the sides, thread the needle through it, and then back up through the first five.

5 Pull all the beads up to the bunka, draw up the thread, and take a small stitch in the bunka, making sure the needle ends up at the back of it.

6 Take another small stitch, bringing the needle out a short distance away – not less than the width of the largest bead (not counting the bugle bead).

7 Anchor the thread with one more small stitch.

8 Repeat steps 4–7 until the length of the beaded fringe is the same as the bunka you used to measure the lampshade.

SHOP-BOUGHT ITEMS CAN BE ADAPTED AND DRESSED UP WITH HOME-MADE DECORATIONS

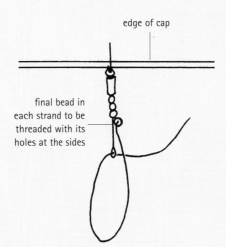

edge of cap

final bead in each strand to be threaded with its holes at the sides

ATTACHING THE BEAD TASSELS

9 Cut the beaded bunka free of the loom and glue it around the bottom edge of the lampshade. A strong PVA is adequate for this.

Decorative trimmings

Cords, pompons, tassels and fringes have all been used for decoration for centuries. Tassels tend to be reserved for curtain tie-backs today, but during the Elizabethan era they were commonly used on clothing and accessories. Equally, while cords, pompons and fringes are now associated mainly with soft furnishings, they were all once used on clothing.

A SMALL SAMPLE OF THE COLOURS AVAILABLE IN EMBROIDERY COTTONS

EQUIPMENT AND MATERIALS
Scissors
Adhesive
Stiff card

THREADS

When I refer to a single strand of embroidery cotton, I am referring to one of the six strands that the manufacturer has spun to make the thread. Embroidery cotton tends to be a little stiff after the winding needed to make cords; this can be a problem when they are added to a fabric intended to have a soft drape, but is fine if they are used for upholstery trim. Silk threads give a softer finish, which is better for applying trimmings to clothing as they will not alter the drape of the fabric. Best of all is Japanese braiding thread (Biron); this is made from rayon and gives a beautiful, soft, shiny cord. However, it can be a little tricky to handle when making tassels and is not suitable for making pompons. As the threads are very slippery, they are difficult to control when winding around the washers: they try to unwind themselves.

BIRON THREADS GIVE A BEAUTIFUL SHINE BUT CAN BE DIFFICULT TO WORK WITH

stiff card

slot

small slits

MY SIMPLE TASSEL-MAKING GADGET

TASSEL-MAKING GADGET

This simple card gadget makes the 'mass production' of tassels easy.

1 Cut two pieces of stiff card, 20 × 3cm (8 × ¼in), for the tassel-making gadget.

2 In each piece, cut a slot 1 × 18cm (⅜ × 7in).

3 Glue both pieces of card together: this will add strength to the gadget.

4 Cut six small slits along the bottom edge, an equal distance apart. The ends of the threads will be anchored in these.

POMPONS

Making pompons is incredibly simple and quick. Any cotton thread can be used, but try to avoid synthetic fibres as they tend to be too springy to stay in place as you work. Crewel wool gives very soft and light pompons that look great as decorative edgings on cushions and furniture; tapestry wool is too thick. I use metal washers as formers rather than card, as they hold their shape, don't tear and won't get snipped when I cut the pompons free.

1 Thread a fine sewing needle with a single strand of embroidery cotton, about 18in (50cm) long.

2 Tie the end of the thread to a pair of washers, placed together, through their central holes.

3 Wrap the thread around the washer until the central hole is filled, then tie it off. (For a smaller pompon, continue wrapping the thread only until the washer is covered.)

4 Using a sharp craft knife, cut the threads around the outer edge. Make sure all the threads are cut or the washers will not separate.

5 Gently prise the washers apart a little and tie a length of invisible thread between them. Pull the thread as tight as possible (without breaking it) and tie a second knot to secure.

6 Remove both washers, then squash and roll the pompon into a nice shape. Trim if necessary.

POMPONS ADD COLOUR AND TEXTURE TO FURNISHINGS AND FABRICS

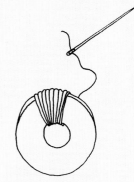

wrapping thread around the washers

continue winding until the hole has been filled

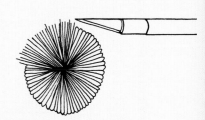

cutting the threads of the pompon

MAKING COTTON POMPONS

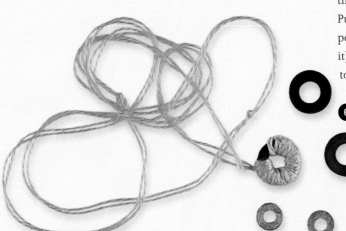

THE SIZE OF THE WASHER, AND THE AMOUNT OF THREAD USED, WILL DETERMINE THE SIZE OF THE FINISHED POMPON

Small hook (a wire hook
from a net curtain
is suitable)

Hobby size manual hand drill*

Scissors

Cotton threads

☙☙

* You can use a full-size drill but you'll
probably find that it is too heavy and
unwieldy to hold for long periods of
time; electric drills are too fast to
count and control the twists

CORDS

I have made cords using just about every type of thread.
I used embroidery cotton for the cords shown here, for no
other reason than almost everyone interested in textiles has
some embroidery cottons in their workbox. Before you
begin you must decide whether to use a single colour,
two or even three different colours, and which colours
you wish to use. This will determine how many strands
of thread you need and how thick the finished cord will
be. For the purpose of simplicity, I have used two strands,
each of two colours.

A SMALL SELECTION FROM MY TANGLE OF THREADS

A HOBBY-SIZE MANUAL DRILL
WILL GIVE YOU THE EASE AND
CONTROL REQUIRED FOR TWISTING
THREADS TO MAKE CORD

1 Wind off 2m (2yds) of cotton for each colour – the length is not critical.

2 Draw out two strands from each.

3 Tie each pair of strands, without mixing the colours, to a suitable stationary object (a drawer handle, for instance). Set aside one pair.

4 Set your hook into the drill, then tie the free ends of the other pair of strands to this. Put a little tension on the threads and wind the drill about 250 times in a clockwise direction. For a softer, looser cord wind less, for a firmer cord wind more. Winding 250 times gives a cord suitable for both clothing and upholstery.

5 Keeping the tension on the strands, unhook your new cord from the drill and tape it to a flat surface to prevent it unwinding.

6 Tie your second pair of strands to the hook in the same way and wind them 250 times in a clockwise direction. Leave this pair on the hook.

7 Keeping the tension on the second pair, tie the first pair back onto the hook, then wind both pairs in an anticlockwise direction, about 150 times.

8 Remove both pairs from the hook and knot all the ends together to prevent them unravelling.

9 Cut the other ends free of their anchor point and knot them.

10 Hold the cord at the centre and allow any overwind to unravel. Your cord is now ready for use.

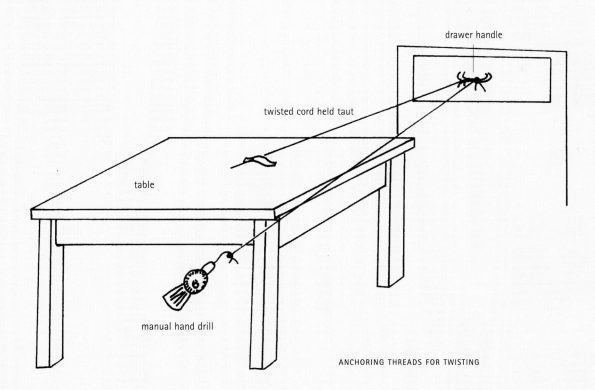

drawer handle

twisted cord held taut

table

manual hand drill

ANCHORING THREADS FOR TWISTING

Tassel-making gadget

Scissors

Cotton threads

TASSELS

To make these tassels you will need cords, in the colours you require, already made. As with cords, tassels can be made with single or multiple colours. The length of cord required depends on the final purpose of the tassels; I've restricted the cord length to 4cm (1½in) for these practice samples. To make a smaller tassel, halve the number of times the threads are wound around the tassel-making gadget and cut the finished tassel shorter. Alternatively, use a finer thread and cut it shorter.

1 Cut six pieces of cord, each 4cm (1½in) long, knot them tightly at both ends, then trim the threads close to the knots. Set these six lengths aside.

2 Cut each thread to 45cm (18in). Use two single strands if you want a tassel of just one colour and a single strand of each colour if you want multicoloured tassels.

3 Pair the threads and wrap them around the card gadget 10 times before securing the end in the slit.

4 Fold the previously prepared cords in half. Carefully, with the point of your scissors, push the knots of the cords between the gadget and the wound threads, just below the centre point.

5 Tie a matching single thread around the middle of the wound threads. Make sure that the tie has caught the cords above the knots and is tight.

6 Put across the threads at the top and bottom. Be careful not to cut the cords as well.

7 Wiggle the cord gently to get into the centre of the threads, then start folding the threads back away from the cords.

8 When all the threads have been folded back, roll the tassel between your thumb and index finger while gently pulling the cord loop: this will even out the threads.

9 With a contrasting thread – if you have used more than one colour to make the tassel, perhaps the lighter coloured thread – wind around the top of the tassel, just below the bump made by the cord knots; six winds are sufficient. Tie the two ends of the winding thread tightly to secure, and trim close to the knot.

10 Trim the bottom of the tassel level and to the length required.

WITH ALL THE THREADS AVAILABLE, THE CHOICE OF COLOUR AND CONTRAST FOR TASSELS IS ENDLESS

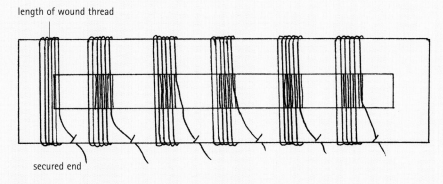

length of wound thread

secured end

THE THREADS WRAPPED AROUND THE CARD GADGET

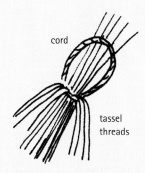

cord

tassel
threads

FOLDING THE THREADS BACK AWAY
FROM THE CORD

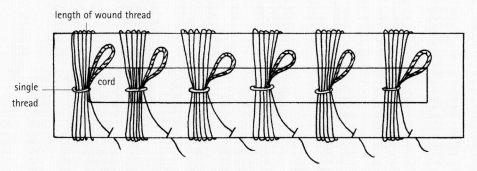

length of wound thread

single
thread

cord

TYING THE MIDDLE OF THE WOUND THREADS

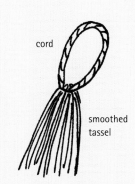

cord

smoothed
tassel

THE CORD SEPARATED FROM
THE TASSEL

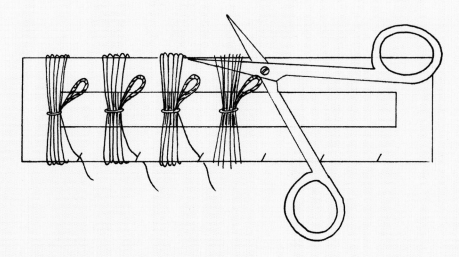

CUTTING THE TOP AND BOTTOM OF THE WOUND THREADS

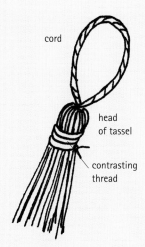

cord

head
of tassel

contrasting
thread

FORMING THE TASSEL HEAD

FRINGES

This is a simple method for making fringes. The warp
threads must be very tight, so it's a good idea to use a
strong thread – silk is preferable, being stronger, finer
and smoother than cotton. Whatever thread you use, it
won't be seen in the finished fringe. If you don't have a
bead loom it is possible to make the fringe using two
upright sticks clamped to a workbench. However, a loom
is preferable as it allows you to get the warp really tight –
and as it is portable, you can work wherever you wish.

You can always incorporate other colours in the weave
or add tassels. You could even embroider into the heading
weave with contrasting colours or cords.

FRINGES ARE OFTEN USED TO DECORATE FURNISHINGS,
CURTAINS, SHAWLS AND OTHER ITEMS OF CLOTHING

1 Warp the loom following the sequence shown. The top three warps should be 3mm (⅛in) apart and the single warp, number 1, should be 20mm (¾in) from warp number 2.

2 Thread a long sewing needle with your chosen thread and tie the other end of the thread to warp 1.

3 Following the sequence given, start on the right and take the needle as follows:

A under 2, over 3, under 4
B over 4, under 3, under 2
C over 2, over 3, under 4
D over 4, over 3, under 2, under 1 E over 1, then repeat from A until the length you require has been woven.

4 Push the weaving close as you progress, but not so close that you crowd the stitches.

5 When you have worked a long enough piece of fringing, either cut warp thread 1 and draw it from the fringe or trim the fringe to the depth required; this is best done while the fringe is still stretched on the loom.

6 The finished fringe should be quite firm at the top but if you wish, you can paint the woven band with a mixture of one part PVA to one part water.

---

warp thread 4

warp thread 3

warp thread 2

warp thread 1

THE WARPING SEQUENCE

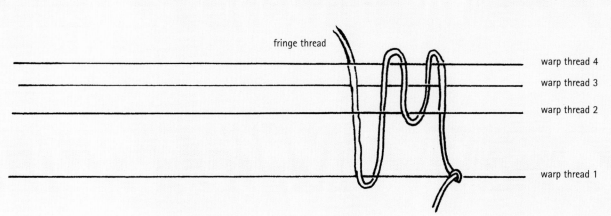

fringe thread

warp thread 4

warp thread 3

warp thread 2

warp thread 1

THE WEAVING SEQUENCE

Tatting

atting is the art of making lace by knotting thread with the aid of a hand shuttle. The technique uses only one stitch; this is worked in two parts and forms an open-textured lace. I recommend practising with No. 20 crochet cotton before embarking on a miniature: this weight will allow you to see the formation of the stitch more clearly.

Tatting requires threads that are smooth and firm, with no elasticity: with an elastic thread it would not be possible to make the knots flip over – an integral part of tatting. However, given this restriction, all weights of thread are suitable for miniature work. The threads I have listed here range from the thickest (DMC spécial dentelles, No. 80) to the finest (Egyptian gassed cotton, No. 170).

In tatting, the use of a finer thread will reduce the final size of the project. This lends itself very well to using full-size patterns designed for thicker thread: use a fine thread and they will automatically reduce in size. Unlike many other arts and crafts, it is no more difficult to tat in miniature than to tat full size because you can feel the stitch being formed. The only equipment you need is a tatting shuttle and a fine crochet hook.

THE SMOOTH, STRONG THREADS OF MADEIRA TANNE
ARE WELL SUITED TO TATTING

INSTRUCTIONS

Tatting instructions are usually written in an abbreviated form like this: 4ds, 1p, 4ds, 1p, 4ds join to last picot of prev. ring, 3ds, 1p, 4ds, 1p. 4ds. Close ring. I have written instructions out in full so you can concentrate on what your hands are doing without having to decipher abbreviations. I have also added explanations; these will not be found on commercial designs.

FILLING THE SHUTTLE

Tatting is worked from a shuttle and a ball or reel of thread. Occasionally patterns will instruct you to 'tie shuttle and ball threads together'; unless you are using two colours, it is pointless to separate the thread wound onto the shuttle from the ball in the first instance, though subsequent rows will need to be tied.

Tie your thread around the central opening in the middle of the shuttle to prevent it moving while you wind it. Wind the thread around the central opening straight from the ball. Do not cut the thread free. The thread must pass through the pointed ends of the shuttle; this will give an audible click with each pass.

Some shuttles have a separate spool. If your shuttle is of this type, remove the spool; it will pop out with a little pressure. To make it easier to wind, push the pointed end of a pencil into the hole in the centre of the spool.

Continue winding until you have sufficient thread on the shuttle; 2m (2yd) is sufficient for most small projects, but wind on more if you intend to make a particularly large or long piece.

METALLIC THREADS CAN MAKE A BOLD DESIGN

BRODER MACHINE THREADS ARE SMOOTH AND STRONG

EGYPTIAN GASSED COTTON GIVES A SMALLER FINISHED PRODUCT

THE ONLY PIECES OF EQUIPMENT YOU NEED FOR TATTING ARE A TATTING SHUTTLE AND A HOOK

SPECIAL DENTELLES ARE THE THICKEST THREADS THAT I USE FOR TATTING

WORKING A STITCH

Wind off 45cm (18in) of thread from the reel. In your left hand, pinch the thread between your thumb and index finger and spread your other three fingers as shown. Wind the thread once around your spread fingers and pinch it again with your thumb and index finger to form a loop of thread.

Pass the shuttle over the top of your left hand to form a loose loop, then pass it under the ring of thread around your fingers and up through the loop that you have just formed. This movement is vital to the success of the stitch. At the same time, lower the middle finger of your left hand slightly and tighten the shuttle thread horizontally in your right hand. These movements may take a little practice. The knot just worked should flip over onto the ring of thread in your left hand.

When the transfer is made correctly, the loop should be able to slide along the ring thread when you extend your middle finger to tighten it. The knot will also tighten up. Slide it along to where your thumb and index finger are pinching the ring thread and hold it there.

Now for the second part of the stitch. Pass the shuttle from the top, through the back of the ring of thread on your left hand and through the loop formed by the shuttle thread. Relax your middle finger as before and tighten the shuttle thread to flip the knot, then extend your middle finger and slide the knot along the thread until it is beside the first knot. This completes one double stitch.

Practise by making a series of double stitches, holding each between the thumb and index finger of your left hand as it is worked. As you use up the thread from the shuttle, simply unwind more. The ring of thread around your left hand will reduce in size as it is used up; enlarge this by stretching the fingers of your left hand to draw more thread from the ball or reel. If any or all of the stitches cease to slide freely, one of your knots has transferred incorrectly. The knots can be undone with the aid of a pin.

WORKING WITH THE BALL THREAD AND THE SHUTTLE THREAD BOTH ATTACHED

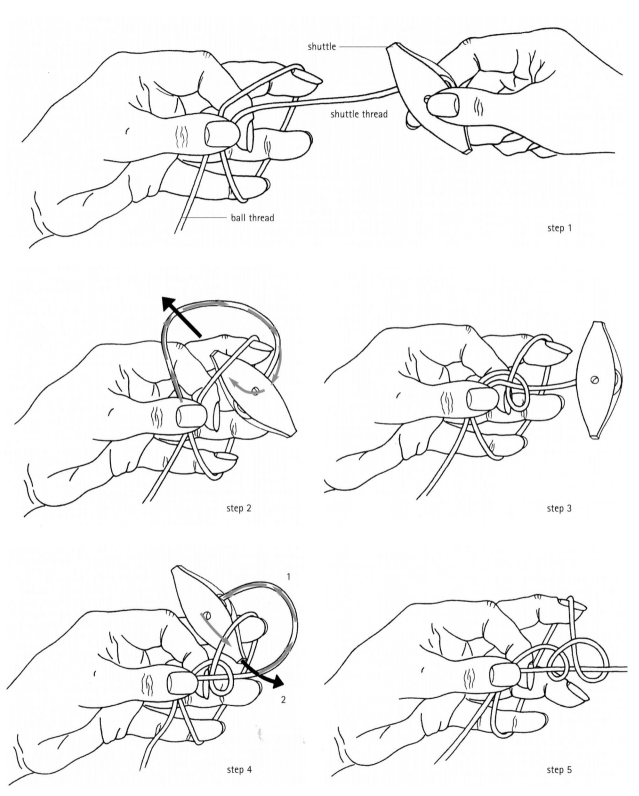

shuttle

shuttle thread

ball thread

step 1

step 2

step 3

step 4

step 5

WORKING A SINGLE STITCH OF TATTING

FORMING A PICOT

Leave a small space between one double stitch and the next. Sliding this completed double stitch along the thread will form a loop. This is known as a picot. Picots can be used decoratively or to make a join (see Joining motifs, p 114). For practice, work six double stitches, one picot, then six more double stitches, release the ring from your left hand and gently pull the shuttle thread to close the ring tightly. If the ring refuses to close, one of the transfer flips is at fault.

FORMING A CHAIN

Pinch the thread between the thumb and index finger of your left hand as above but this time, instead of forming a ring, wind the same thread around the little finger of your left hand, stretching the thread only across the back of your fingers. Work the double stitches as before, sliding them along to be pinched between your thumb and index finger. This will result in the stitches lying side by side on a length of thread but instead of tightening into a ring, they will form a gentle curve.

When patterns mention 'reverse work' it usually means that a chain will follow. After the ring has been tightened, simply turn it over so that the reel/ball thread is on the right-hand side of the part just worked. Remember to return the work to its original position after the chain has been worked – this instruction may not always be given in the pattern you are following.

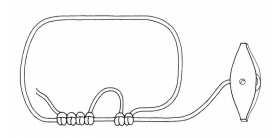

FORMING A PICOT

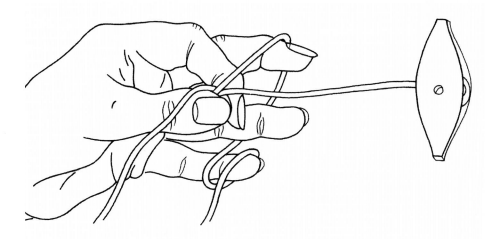

FORMING A CHAIN

WORKING TO SCALE

These four samples were worked using threads of different sizes. The largest was worked with spécial dentelles, No. 80. The design worked in this particular thread is too big for use in miniatures. The second sample was worked in Madeira tanne, No. 50. Along with Broder machine, No. 50, this is my preferred thread for tatting and lace making: both are smooth and strong and give a predictable result. The third sample was worked in Egyptian gassed cotton, No. 120, and the fourth in Egyptian gassed cotton, No. 170. Both of these threads approach true miniature scale.

This is the smallest work you can produce with cotton threads, and the pieces require very delicate handling. It is possible to get a finer lace using the much stronger silk threads and Japanese braiding threads (Biron). The working methods are the same as for cotton but the threads are harder to control; you must take care to ensure that the knots flip properly.

IN TATTING, THE THICKNESS OF THE THREAD USED HAS
A DIRECT IMPACT ON THE SIZE OF THE FINISHED PIECE

JOINING MOTIFS

Most, if not all designs require motifs to be joined. This is done using the picots you have worked and a hook – either the one supplied with your shuttle or a crochet hook. The best way to explain how to join motifs is to work through a sample pattern.

Wind your shuttle with No. 20 crochet cotton. Work a ring of four double stitches, one picot, four double stitches, one picot, four double stitches. Close the ring.

Work the first four double stitches of a second ring, then join these to the last picot worked on the previous ring by inserting a hook down through that picot and drawing up a loop of thread from the ring of thread around your left hand; pull up enough to form a loop large enough to pass the shuttle through. The fingers of your left hand will close when you pull the loop up; after passing the shuttle through this loop, open your fingers again to pull the loop down. Treat this loop as the first half of a double stitch, and continue to work the second half.

Complete the ring by working three double stitches, one picot and four double stitches, then close the ring.

AN EDGING PATTERN

This design is very simple and open, which makes it easy and quick to work. Occasionally, when working an edging pattern, a foundation row of crochet will be used to work the tatting onto but this design is worked without such a foundation. It uses both ball and shuttle thread, leaving the shuttle thread connected to the ball or reel.

A ROW OF MOTIFS WORKED TO FORM A DECORATIVE EDGING

1 Wind your chosen thread onto the shuttle.

2 Work the first part by making a ring of four double stitches, one picot, and four double stitches. Close the ring (draw closed by pulling the shuttle thread) and reverse the work (turn the ring just made).

3 For the second part, make a chain of three double stitches, one picot, two double stitches, then one picot, nine times, then add a further three double stitches. (The chain will have three double stitches and a total of 10 picots, each separated by two double stitches, with three double stitches to finish.)

4 Reverse the work.

5 The third part is a ring of eight double stitches. Join this to the corresponding picot of the first ring (there are two picots on the first ring worked; use the one on the right). Work a further four double stitches, one picot and four double stitches. Close the ring.

6 Work the fourth part by making a ring of four double stitches, one picot, four double stitches, one picot and four double stitches. Close the ring.

7 Reverse the work.

8 For the fifth part of the pattern, make a chain of three double stitches. Join this to the last picot of the previous chain, then make two double stitches and one picot nine times, followed by three double stitches.

9 Repeat the third, fourth and fifth parts until you have reached the desired length for your edging.

10 Tie the threads together and cut.

ABOUT THE AUTHOR

The textile arts have been a part of my life for as long as I can remember. I had knitting needles the same as my mother's and grandmother's but half as long and was able to knit and crochet before I went to school, knitting mittens when the other children were knitting squares and pot holders. I was also taught embroidery and sewing at home. For most of my life I took these skills for granted and didn't consider them a career option; instead I trained as a nurse. I continued sewing and knitting in my spare time, adding new skills all the time, but it wasn't until poor health ended my nursing career that I began to look at my skills as a means of earning a living.

I learned to spin to make one-ply wool for Shetland lace shawls and christening gowns. The natural progression from this was to add colour to the wool. By this time I had also discovered miniatures and was knocked out by the range and quality of what was on offer. Spinning very fine wool for knitting shawls, I thought it would look wonderful used to embroider a miniature carpet for my dolls' house. I had already made several full-sized rugs dyed with commercial dyes, and a few miniature rugs using embroidery cotton. In both cases I was dissatisfied with the harsh colours, so I decided to dye the wool using natural materials – but first I had to learn how to do it. What followed were months of research and experimentation and a few disasters on the way. I've stained my tiled floor with boil-over dye baths and produced terrible smells that caused my family to evacuate the house and caused me a huge amount of work: every article made of fabric had to be washed to remove the smell. I was threatened with banishment to the garden if I created any more bad smells. Needless to say, I never used that particular plant again. The best day was when I gathered an audience in the garden to view my indigo vat. When wool comes out of an indigo bath it is a dirty yellow, but hang it on a washing line in the sunshine and it turns a wonderful blue. My neighbours were fascinated with the whole process. However, an indigo vat is also smelly: indigo will only work in deoxygenated water – in other words, it must be stagnant.

By the time I had perfected dyeing, I had amassed a large range of colours plus some very interesting variegated wool from dyes not being taken up evenly. This is a very common problem for beginners, but the wool should not be thrown away: I've never seen an antique carpet in which the colour was even. I worked my wools into carpets and the results were well worth the effort. Unfortunately, they were so much admired that I now have none myself. With dyeing perfected I moved on to applying colour to other textiles, which opened the door to techniques such as screen printing. I went to college to learn about textiles from the experts but only lasted about three months. The course was not what I expected; they were teaching skills that I already had, so I spent a lot of time helping other students when lecturers disappeared. The consensus of opinion from my peers and lecturers was that I should be passing on my skills, not re-covering old ground. Hence this book. I hope you enjoy trying out the techniques within and are encouraged by your results to continue to a more advanced level.

INDEX

TITLES AVAILABLE FROM GMC PUBLICATIONS

BOOKS

WOODCARVING

Beginning Woodcarving   *GMC Publications*
Carving Architectural Detail in Wood: The Classical Tradition
                                                       Frederick Wilbur
Carving Birds & Beasts   *GMC Publications*
Carving the Human Figure: Studies in Wood and Stone
                                                       Dick Onians
Carving Nature: Wildlife Studies in Wood   *Frank Fox-Wilson*
Carving on Turning   *Chris Pye*
Decorative Woodcarving   *Jeremy Williams*
Elements of Woodcarving   *Chris Pye*
Essential Woodcarving Techniques   *Dick Onians*
Lettercarving in Wood: A Practical Course   *Chris Pye*
Making & Using Working Drawings for Realistic Model Animals
                                                       Basil F. Fordham
Power Tools for Woodcarving   *David Tippey*
Relief Carving in Wood: A Practical Introduction   *Chris Pye*
Understanding Woodcarving in the Round   *GMC Publications*
Useful Techniques for Woodcarvers   *GMC Publications*
Woodcarving: A Foundation Course   *Zoë Gertner*
Woodcarving for Beginners   *GMC Publications*
Woodcarving Tools, Materials & Equipment (New Edition)
                                                       Chris Pye

WOODTURNING

Adventures in Woodturning   *David Springett*
Bert Marsh: Woodturner   *Bert Marsh*
Bowl Turning Techniques Masterclass   *Tony Boase*
Colouring Techniques for Woodturners   *Jan Sanders*
Contemporary Turned Wood: New Perspectives in a Rich Tradition
                              Ray Leier, Jan Peters & Kevin Wallace
The Craftsman Woodturner   *Peter Child*
Decorating Turned Wood: The Maker's Eye*Liz & Michael O'Donnell*
Decorative Techniques for Woodturners   *Hilary Bowen*
Illustrated Woodturning Techniques   *John Hunnex*
Intermediate Woodturning Projects   *GMC Publications*
Keith Rowley's Woodturning Projects   *Keith Rowley*
Making Screw Threads in Wood   *Fred Holder*

Turned Boxes: 50 Designs   *Chris Stott*
Turning Green Wood   *Michael O'Donnell*
Turning Pens and Pencils   *Kip Christensen & Rex Burningham*
Useful Woodturning Projects   *GMC Publications*
Woodturning: Bowls, Platters, Hollow Forms, Vases, Vessels,
Bottles, Flasks, Tankards, Plates   *GMC Publications*
Woodturning: A Foundation Course (New Edition) *Keith Rowley*
Woodturning: A Fresh Approach   *Robert Chapman*
Woodturning: An Individual Approach   *Dave Regester*
Woodturning: A Source Book of Shapes   *John Hunnex*
Woodturning Jewellery   *Hilary Bowen*
Woodturning Masterclass   *Tony Boase*
Woodturning Techniques   *GMC Publications*

WOODWORKING

Advanced Scrollsaw Projects   *GMC Publications*
Beginning Picture Marquetry   *Lawrence Threadgold*
Bird Boxes and Feeders for the Garden   *Dave Mackenzie*
Complete Woodfinishing   *Ian Hosker*
David Charlesworth's Furniture-Making Techniques
                                                       David Charlesworth
David Charlesworth's Furniture-Making Techniques – Volume 2
                                                       David Charlesworth
The Encyclopedia of Joint Making   *Terrie Noll*
Furniture-Making Projects for the Wood Craftsman
                                                       GMC Publications
Furniture-Making Techniques for the Wood Craftsman
                                                       GMC Publications
Furniture Restoration (Practical Crafts)   *Kevin Jan Bonner*
Furniture Restoration: A Professional at Work   *John Lloyd*
Furniture Restoration and Repair for Beginners *Kevin Jan Bonner*
Furniture Restoration Workshop   *Kevin Jan Bonner*
Green Woodwork   *Mike Abbott*
Intarsia: 30 Patterns for the Scrollsaw   *John Everett*
Kevin Ley's Furniture Projects   *Kevin Ley*
Making Chairs and Tables   *GMC Publications*
Making Chairs and Tables – Volume 2   *GMC Publications*
Making Classic English Furniture   *Paul Richardson*
Making Heirloom Boxes   *Peter Lloyd*
Making Little Boxes from Wood   *John Bennett*
Making Screw Threads in Wood   *Fred Holder*
Making Shaker Furniture   *Barry Jackson*

UPHOLSTERY

TOYMAKING

DOLLS' HOUSES AND MINIATURES

CRAFTS

VIDEOS

Drop-in and Pinstuffed Seats	*David James*	Twists and Advanced Turning	*Dennis White*
Stuffover Upholstery	*David James*	Sharpening the Professional Way	*Jim Kingshott*
Elliptical Turning	*David Springett*	Sharpening Turning & Carving Tools	*Jim Kingshott*
Woodturning Wizardry	*David Springett*	Bowl Turning	*John Jordan*
Turning Between Centres: The Basics	*Dennis White*	Hollow Turning	*John Jordan*
Turning Bowls	*Dennis White*	Woodturning: A Foundation Course	*Keith Rowley*
Boxes, Goblets and Screw Threads	*Dennis White*	Carving a Figure: The Female Form	*Ray Gonzalez*
Novelties and Projects	*Dennis White*	The Router: A Beginner's Guide	*Alan Goodsell*
Classic Profiles	*Dennis White*	The Scroll Saw: A Beginner's Guide	*John Burke*

MAGAZINES

WOODTURNING ◆ WOODCARVING

FURNITURE & CABINETMAKING

THE ROUTER ◆ WOODWORKING ◆ THE DOLLS' HOUSE MAGAZINE

OUTDOOR PHOTOGRAPHY

BLACK & WHITE PHOTOGRAPHY

MACHINE KNITTING NEWS

BUSINESSMATTERS

The above represents a full list of all titles currently published or scheduled to be published.
All are available direct from the Publishers or through bookshops, newsagents and specialist retailers.
To place an order, or to obtain a complete catalogue, contact:

GMC Publications, Castle Place
166 High Street Lewes
East Sussex BN7 1XU
United Kingdom
Tel: 01273 488005
Fax: 01273 478606
E-mail: pubs@thegmcgroup.com

Orders by credit card are accepted